The Scots Philosophical Monograph Series

While this monograph series is published on behalf of the Scots Philosophical Club, refereed by a panel of distinguished philosophers in the Club, and has as one of its aims the provision of a publishing outlet for philosophical work being done in Scotland, it is nevertheless international. The Club hopes to bring out original works, written in a lively and readable style, and devoted to central areas of current philosophical concern, from philosophers working anywhere in the world.

As a deliberate policy we have specified no areas of the subject on which the series is to concentrate. The emphasis is on originality rather than, say, on surveys of literature, commentaries on the work of others, or exegesis. Historical works will be included only in so far as they also contribute significantly to topical debates.

As well as our debt to the referees and consulting editors, we have to acknowledge a very real debt to the universities of Glasgow, Edinburgh, Aberdeen, Stirling and St Andrews who—despite the current stringencies—have given financial support to the series.

Series Editors: Andrew Brennan, William Lyons

Consulting Editors:

J R Cameron *Aberdeen*
Neil Cooper *Dundee*
Robin Downie *Glasgow*
R W Hepburn *Edinburgh*
Bernard Mayo *St Andrews*
Neil Tennant *Stirling*
Crispin Wright *St Andrews*

Scots Philosophical Monographs Number Five

UNDERSTANDING
IDENTITY STATEMENTS

Scots Philosophical Monographs

Scots Philosophical Monographs Number Five

UNDERSTANDING IDENTITY STATEMENTS
THOMAS V MORRIS

Series Editors *Andrew Brennan & William Lyons*

ABERDEEN UNIVERSITY PRESS

First published 1984
Aberdeen University Press
A member of the Pergamon Group

British Library Cataloguing in Publication Data

Morris, Thomas V.
Understanding identity statements
(Scots philosophical monographs, ISSN 0144-3062; 5)
1. Identity
I. Title   II. Series
149'.943   BD236

ISBN 0-08-030388-9
ISBN 0-08-030389-7 Pbk

PRINTED IN GREAT BRITAIN AT
ABERDEEN UNIVERSITY PRESS

Contents

Preface

Identity statements recently have come to be of significant interest to many philosophers, and rightly so. For they are an important form of statement in any natural language. In this study, I attempt to put some of the basic philosophical issues they raise in a fresh perspective and to provide some of the fundamental elements of an overall view of identity and identity statements. Because I think the topics to be of some general importance, I have presented my arguments in such a way as to make them intelligible to a broader audience than just aficionados of contemporary philosophy of language and initiates into the esoterica of analytic metaphysics. I have kept the text as simple as the subject matter allows, leaving aside much technical jargon and many needless complexities, so that anyone with even a modicum of familiarity with logic, or the style of argument current in philosophy, can follow the exposition. And for the reader who lacks mastery of the relevant literatures, I have provided extensive references, as well as liberally using quotations from others whose work is relevant to my case. By these devices, the reader easily can attain a clear view of how my own concerns are situated in a broader range of work in contemporary philosophy, and can be led on to further work himself.

I began to develop the understanding of identity statements articulated in this study during the spring of 1977. Some of the ideas were defended, and thereby refined, in long and enjoyable conversations with Thomas Morawetz, Robert Jaeger, and Jorge Garcia. To them I owe a great deal. And were it not for the encouragement of Neil Delaney, I might never have prepared my arguments for publication. Special thanks also go to Robert Fogelin, Michael Williams, Ruth Marcus, and Scott Soames. Various of their opinions and positions on the topics treated here have affected what I have to say. Finally, I would like to express my gratitude to my wife Mary, for her labour of typing the inaugural draft of this essay. To her it is dedicated.

Thomas V Morris
The University of Notre Dame
Indiana

. . . despite its simplicity, identity invites confusion. W V Quine

The notion of 'is' used in the sense of strict identity is none too clear.
D L Gunner

. . . the connection between the properties attributed to identity by formal logic, and our everyday conception of identity, is not clear, and may seem even quite puzzling. John Perry

The identity relation is not a stranger to philosophical trouble.
John Woods

The little word 'is' is perhaps for philosophers the most troublesome in the language. John Hick

No wonder, then, that reflection on identity and sameness ends, often and quickly, in confusion and puzzlement. H N Castañeda

. . . whole books can and must be written about the principle of identity. . . .
Karl Rahner

Introduction

A few years ago, Saul Kripke observed that 'Statements of identity should seem very simple, but they are somehow very puzzling to philosophers'.[1] It will be a goal of this study to explain some of that puzzlement and display some of that simplicity.

Identity statements indeed should seem very simple. Every competent user of the English language, for example, has in his linguistic repertoire such expressions as 'identity', 'the same', 'is identical with', and 'is the same as', as well as the appropriate use of the verb 'to be', flanked by two referring expressions. We all can make and understand identity statements. But rarely has such a common form of expression caused so much trouble and aroused so much discussion among philosophers. In this regard, identity statements rank in the same category as, say, negative existentials. We have no trouble at all understanding them, but have quite a time trying to arrive at a *philosophical* understanding of them, and of our ordinary grasp of them. This philosophical perplexity is certainly something to be reckoned with.

Most contemporary philosophers seem to hold that one or the other of two well known alternative analyses gives an accurate account of the propositional content of identity statements. The more traditional of these recently has experienced a resurgence of popularity among the most respected of present day logicians and metaphysicians. I shall call it 'the objectual analysis'. According to it, an identity statement asserts that a certain property is had by whatever is referred to as the subject of the statement. This is the quite unique property of standing in the relation of identity, or of being self-identical. In chapter one, I consider this analysis and a serious problem it faces. After giving a hearing to its most eminent defenders, I find it wanting.

The other analysis found its seminal expression in the early work of Frege, and has had many influential proponents. I shall call it 'the metalinguistic analysis'. According to this account, an identity statement asserts that a certain relation holds between whatever two referring expressions are used in making the statement. This is basically the relation

[1] Notes start on p 139

of co-referentiality, or as Frege puts its, of 'naming the same thing'. In chapter two I examine what I consider to be the most persuasive form of this analysis. In doing so, I suggest a controversial thesis concerning Frege's own position. Although my overall argument does not stand or fall on this thesis, the presentation of it illuminates some aspects of a well developed metalinguistic analysis which otherwise easily are overlooked. In spite of the insights provided by this analysis, I find it also wanting.

In chapter three, I consider briefly the dilemma philosophers have faced in feeling forced to choose between these two problematic analyses, each of which has its obvious faults. I suggest why it has been thought that these are the only two options available to us as accounts of identity statements. It may well be that a particular philosophical method, and one major assumption concerning these statements, have conspired to create this dilemma. Briefly put, the method is to start with an analysis of the notion of identity, and to bring the results of this analysis to bear on the analysis of identity statements. The assumption is that there is an answer to the question : What does an identity statement state?

Without going into any detail here, I should indicate that in chapter four I reverse the method and reject the assumption. An attempt is made to arrive at a philosophical understanding of identity statements by examining how they function in ordinary human discourse and contribute to our empirical knowledge. Whereas philosophers have tried to specify a determinate cognitive content for identity statements and have failed, I present instead what I call a 'functional account' of these statements, which explicates their informative import in terms of their standard epistemic function.

In chapter five, I clarify and defend my own approach to understanding identity statements. Some elements of an overall account of identity and identity statements are sketched out, their inter-relations are displayed, and the consistency of the resultant view is established. With this chapter, the main arguments of part one come to completion.

From chapters three, four, and five, it should become clear that this essay is not primarily about the *notion* or concept of identity, but is rather mainly focussed on *identity statements*. From this perspective, I take a look in chapter six at a group of principles often known loosely and collectively as 'Leibniz's Law'. It is common to hear it said that Leibniz's Law 'governs' identity. By this it usually is meant that those, or at least one of those, principles, along with other principles of reflexivity, symmetry, and transitivity, define the notion of identity and serve as criteria for its holding in any given case. Thus Leibniz's Law is thought to explicate the notion of identity.

This is not my approach. I look at the principles involved as they relate to identity statements. It is suggested that, correctly understood, they indicate the conditions under which we are warranted in asserting or accepting identities, and reveal the way in which these statements function epistemically. Thus, what I, in deference to tradition, continue to call 'Leibniz's Law' provides for our assessment of identity statements.

At the end of chapter six, I consider a range of important but apparently deviant identity statements often called 'cross-category identities'. Many philosophers have held that such statements express significant metaphysical truth in spite of their obvious violation of Leibniz's Law as traditionally formulated. I suggest that this claim can be made plausible only if it can be argued on general grounds that an emendation or restriction of Leibniz's Law is needed, and the reformulated version will allow the truth of these identities.

In chapter seven I sketch out the kind of general theory which alone would undergird and warrant such a reformulation of Leibniz's Law. For reasons presented there, I call it 'the theory of regulative identity'. In its broad outlines, I believe it is a relatively attractive position. It embodies the viewpoint, increasingly popular this century, that the presence of a certain kind of conceptual multiplicity in natural languages need not be taken to imply a correspondingly manifold ontology.

However, in the eighth chapter, I evaluate the theory and find it attended by serious and probably insurmountable difficulties. A look at these problems will make clear to us the logical price of holding any genuinely cross-category identity statements to be true. Some general implications are mentioned for metaphysical positions which incorporate such statements, although these are not discussed in detail.

At the end of chapter eight, it is suggested that the only plausible defence of any apparently cross-category identity statement as a literal statement of numerical identity expressing truth of metaphysical import must involve arguing that, properly understood, it is not a semantically deviant statement standing in violation of the traditional version of Leibniz's Law after all. In chapter nine, the concluding chapter, I examine what has seemed to many people to be the most extraordinary and wildly deviant identity claim ever propounded by serious philosophers, a claim drawn from Christian theology which seems to stand in obvious and even flagrant violation of Leibniz's Law. As a case study in reconciling apparently cross-category identity statements to Leibniz's Law, I show how even this most extreme of examples can be argued to satisfy the standard conditions for the warranted assertion of identities. In addition to the intrinsic interest of this case, it serves to make some general points about our assessment of metaphysically interesting identity statements.

There are many questions about identity not addressed in this book. For example, some philosophers use the word 'identity' often to mean 'self-understanding'. One's identity is one's existential self-understanding. There are said to be many serious problems raised by this conception, but none of them falls within the purview of my study. As will have become clear by now, my concern is broadly logical rather than existential.

There are also some metaphysical questions raised by philosophers in the context of talk about identity with which I shall not deal. These fall into basically two categories. Often it is said that there are two kinds of identity—qualitative and numerical. This distinction can be misleading in either of two ways. First, it often is just a loose way of speaking, since by 'qualitative identity' is meant usually just exact similarity in some or many respects. On the other hand, if more than that is meant by 'qualitative identity', it just amounts to the numerical identity of qualities exemplified by different individuals. Certainly there is such a use of identity expressions (e.g. two automobiles are said to be identical, two samples of paint are said to be the same colour, etc.), and it is believed to raise difficult philosophical problems. These are the age old metaphysical questions concerning universals, which never cease to be interesting to philosophers. These questions, however, fall outside the scope of my study, as I shall be concerned only with statements of numerical identity regarding concrete (i.e. non-abstract) particulars. Outside mathematics, this is the most common sort of identity claim.

The second category of metaphysical questions I shall not discuss arises out of the use of identity expressions to convey the idea of continuity or persistence through time. We can draw a rough distinction between two types of identity statement, 'diachronic' and 'synchronic'. By a diachronic identity statement is meant the assertion of some object's continuity or persistence throughout time and change. A *via negativa* will suffice here for the other side of the distinction. A synchronic identity statement does not have continuity or persistence through time as its point. We can make them without explicit concern about such issues.

Philosophical questions pertaining to diachronic identity statements often are considered under such titles as 'Identity and Spatio-temporal Continuity', and 'Personal Identity'. These are the issues of change, continuity, essential properties, substrata and their accidents, and so forth—metaphysical topics which are outside the bounds of this essay. I am concerned primarily to understand a certain kind of synchronic, numerical identity statement (to employ both distinctions just mentioned). And the issues I address are more properly logical and linguistic than metaphysical in most respects, although their metaphysical implications are far from negligible.

However, there is a sense in which this study is at least as epistemological as it is logical or linguistic in emphasis. For one thing, it does not attempt to take care of everything a work on the relevant logical topics should treat. There is at least one widely discussed logical issue, or more accurately, issue in philosophical logic, concerning identity statements on which I do not attempt to establish a definite conclusion. This is the question about the modality of the truth value of identity statements—whether they are necessary or contingent. Although I do not explicitly attempt to settle this issue, I believe that the overall thrust of what I do say has interesting implications for the question, which should become evident to the careful reader.

But the main reason I say that this essay is as epistemological as logical in orientation should become plain as it is read. Especially in chapters three, four and six, it should be clear that my method of attempting to understand identity statements is very different from that which has been employed by most logicians. It involves looking at how such statements function in human knowledge, and results in an awareness of their epistemic significance.

It should be emphasised that this methodological difference is important. I believe that, as salutary as the development of modern logic has been in most respects, it has inculcated in many of us habits of thinking which do not always yield philosophical perspicacity. This monograph shows one way in which a perspective resulting from such habits has kept philosophers—such prominent practitioners as Frege, Wittgenstein, Tarski, Quine, Plantinga, Kripke, and Stalnaker—from getting clear about a very important class of statements. It is the task of this study to gain a bit of that elusive clarity.

Part One

ANALYSING IDENTITY STATEMENTS

1

The Objectual Analysis

Many philosophers think they have an accurate account of what identity statements state. In this chapter I shall take a look at the analysis which seems to be thought by most to supply that account. In order to provide a focus for my remarks, I should introduce here an example of the kind of sentence whose normal utterance in English is standardly seen as expressing such a statement. The most familiar of examples occurring in the literature on identity usually is presented in roughly the following way.

In ancient times, people who gazed heaven-ward noticed a bright point of light appearing early in the evening sky, which they named 'Hesperus'.[1] They also noticed a bright heavenly body visible in the mornings which they named 'Phosphorus'. For many years, they talked of both Hesperus the evening star and Phosphorus the morning star. But then a startling astronomical discovery was made. It was discovered that Hesperus *is* Phosphorus, that they are one and the same celestial body (known to us now as the planet Venus). One English sentence which can be used to express this discovered fact I shall refer to by the letter 'S', and offer as exemplifying the kind of sentence taken by philosophers to express an identity statement on any standard occurrence of its utterance:

S   Hesperus is Phosphorus.

It is a widespread assumption that a general account can be given of what identity statements state, and that such an account will yield quite easily a determinate content for any particular identity statement. Thus, it is considered altogether appropriate to ask: What is stated by S? And the answer is thought by many to be simple. Currently most philosophers would understand S as stating that a certain relation, that of identity, holds between the object referred to by the term 'Hesperus' and the object referred to by the term 'Phosphorus'. Such an explication of what is stated by S I shall call an 'objectual analysis' of S. It can be seen as a particular application of a general thesis about identity statements:

> Any sentence which expresses an identity statement thereby asserts the holding of the relation of identity between the referent of the subject term and the referent of the predicate nominative term which flank its occurrence of the verb 'to be'.

On this account, an identity statement is a statement *about* the object(s) referred to by the referring expressions with which it is made. It is not in any sense a statement about those expressions themselves. They do not figure in its truth conditions. What the relation in question involves standardly is spelled out by a set of rules, principles, or laws said to 'govern' identity: reflexivity, symmetry, transitivity, and that group of principles known as 'Leibniz's Law'.

This is the basic understanding of identity statements most common among philosophers. It underlies almost every important discussion of identity in the recent literature; yet it is rarely, if ever, explicitly presented or argued as the correct analysis of such statements. It seems rather to be assumed as so obvious that it needs no argument. However, a well known difficulty arises from it. This difficulty is easily seen.

The problem of informative identities

According to this analysis, any instantiation of the identity relation must hold with regard to a single object.[2] For any identity statement will be true only if the subject term and the predicate nominative term of the sentence with which it is made refer not to two different objects, but only to one. Thus identity is said to be a one termed reflexive relation, holding between an object and itself.

If S makes a true statement—which, let us grant, it does—then according to an objectual analysis, what is truly stated is that a particular object (referred to in S by both the name 'Hesperus' and the name 'Phosphorus') bears the relation of identity to itself. But this analysis would also allow us to specify on that condition that S asserts the holding of this relation with regard to the referent of its predicate noun, 'Phosphorus'. And it is interesting to note that according to this analysis, that very same assertion is made by the quite different sentence:

(1)   Phosphorus is Phosphorus

If S predicates of the referent of 'Phosphorus' the relation of identity, or the property of standing in this relation, (1) does also. On this analysis, the truth conditions of the statement made by (1) are exactly the same as those of the statement made by S, namely, the identity of the object we now know as the planet Venus with itself. And on this account, they have no other assertorial content. So it seems we must conclude that S and (1) make the same statement.[3]

And it is at this point that our well known problem appears. (1) is one of those peculiar sentences which have been classified by a great many philosophers as expressing in *some* sense a necessary, *a priori*, and/or analytic truth. Now the notions of necessary, *a priori*, and analytic truth have of course been explicated in various ways (none of which is altogether uncontroversial), but common to them all traditionally has been the idea that such truth properly is ascertained *not* by empirical observations or investigations into how things happen to be in the actual world. It is to be seen merely by attending to and understanding the logical structure and individual terms of the sentence which bears it. Anyone who knows that 'Phosphorus' is an actually referring expression (a name here), and who understands this particular use of the verb 'to be', knows thereby that the statement or proposition expressed by (1) is true. There seems to be no possibility of understanding an utterance of this sentence, knowing what statement it expresses, and still being in doubt as to its truth. In particular, it would seem that no astronomical observation or factual reasoning is needed for the determining of its truth value. Aside from a couple of lexical or semantic facts, no empirical information is relevant to its truth.[4]

But consider this statement as allegedly made by S. If S and (1) make the same statement, it would seem that the truth of what S asserts should be evident once the logical structure and individual terms of that sentence are understood. As our look at (1) made clear, it is that kind of statement. No other factual information should be needed to ascertain its truth. Understanding the meaning of S, knowing what statement it is used to express, should amount to knowing the truth of what it states. But the notorious problem is this: Historically, it was an empirical discovery that the statement made by S is true. Only many long nights of star-gazing, and a solid dose of empirical reasoning could disclose and establish that truth. A knowledge that 'Hesperus' and 'Phosphorus' both are actually referring expressions, and an understanding of this use of the verb 'to be' do not amount to a knowledge that the statement made by S is true.

So according to an objectual analysis, it happens to be the case that S and (1) make the same statement. They carry the same information. But this is counter-intuitive. Surely it is the case neither that (1) is as informative as S nor that S is as uninformative as (1). Yet the dilemma this analysis seems to yield is that of having to hold either that all true identities are uninformative—which is obviously false—or else that all identity statements of the form of (1) (a = a) are informative (and *just as* informative as those of the form of S)—also obviously false.

The difficulty can be stated in another general way. There is a large class of identity statements, the truth of whose members seems to be as-certainable only by empirical methods, and which therefore are empirically informative. But according to an objectual analysis, any sentence which expresses such a statement is to be understood as making the same statement as some other sentence which clearly expresses a truth in some sense non-empirical or non-informative; i.e., in some sense trivially necessary, *a priori*, or analytic. So an objectual analysis of identity statements seems not to account for the informative role of a large class of such statements. But in that case it must be rejected, and some other analysis given.

Let me anticipate briefly one response which might be made at this point. Others will be dealt with subsequently. It has been pointed out by some authors recently that there are circumstances in which sentences of the form of (1) can be uttered to make informative statements, and thus to express the results of some empirical discovery. If this is so, it might be urged, then would not the implication of the objectual analysis that S and (1) make the same statement be less paradoxical or implausible? I believe on the contrary that it can be seen quite easily that the phenomenon in question is strictly irrelevant to the problem of informative identities the objectual account faces.

First, consider the case of a wayward husband. Let us sympathetically imagine the plight of a woman who has tried in vain to reform her husband's socially unbecoming behaviour for years. Suppose that in the company of a close friend who knows of her long and futile struggle, she sees her mate do something particularly stupid, embarrassing to them both. She might shrug her shoulders and say apologetically, 'George is George', thereby conveying the proposition that the man named is acting, un-fortunately, in character, exemplifying behavioural traits which are habitual, or invariable, or ineradicable, and possibly unique to him. As incorrigible as George might be, we surely would not consider his wife's statement a necessary truth in any sense. Nor would it be *a priori*, analytic, trivial, or uninformative for any listener who understood the utterance. This might be thought to suggest the possibility that the implication of the objectual analysis for S and (1) need not be taken to imply that the statement made by S has any of these properties. But this is not so.

The irrelevance of this case to the problem of informative identities should be clear. The utterance in question, although employing a sentence form isomorphic with (1), does not express an identity statement at all. So this story does not present us with a case of a sentence like (1) which clearly does convey an informative identity claim. Lest my denial be taken as dogmatic, I should refer the reader to chapter four where conditions are presented under which and under which alone a sentence is uttered to make an identity statement. The remark about George fails to satisfy one of the conditions. It is in roughly the category of remarks like 'Business is business', or 'War is war'. It might even be seen by a pessimist about husbands to be a present tense instantiation of 'Boys will be boys'. Such utterances have standard contextual meaning, but they are not identity claims. Thus their logical and epistemic characteristics are irrelevant to the problem of informative identities.

Another type of case may seem to come closer to what is needed. Imagine organised crime operating along the waterfront of a major city, run by an absentee boss referred to by his underlings as 'the Governor'. As the head of a task force on organised crime, you have been attempting for months to discover the identity of this king-pin so that you could smash the operation. You receive a telephone call late at night from the state capital. A well placed informant who is a confidant of the head of state says he has the crucial information you have needed, and whispers 'The Governor is the Governor'. Surely this could be an exciting piece of information revealing a startling case of political corruption. And the statement uttered can be taken most plausibly to be an identity statement. So we have here a sentence isomorphic with (1), which conveys an identity statement, and which expresses nothing analytic, trivial, uninformative, *a priori*, or in any sense necessarily true. In fact, the statement expressed is as informative as an identity statement can be. So the implication of the objectual analysis that any true identity of the form of S expresses the same statement as an identity of the form of (1) need not be taken to imply that all true identities are uninformative, and so forth. Nor, on the basis of this case, is the possible implication that there are many identities isomorphic with (1) which are as informative as identities like S an unacceptable one. So it might be thought that the existence of such cases eliminates or undercuts the problem of informative identities as a problem for the objectual analysis. But again this is not so.

A distinction must be drawn between two quite different uses of sentences like 'The Governor is the Governor', sentences isomorphic with (1). When the subject and predicate nouns are tokens of different semantic types as well as being tokens of the same word or phrase type, as in this story, the sentence can be uttered to express an informative identity claim. That is, when tokens of 'the Governor' have been used in two apparently unrelated semantic contexts, on the waterfront and in the state capital, a context can be generated in which an utterance of 'The Governor is the Governor' does convey empirical information, linking the two previously distinct usages. Contrast such a case with circumstances in which we employ merely the rule of reflexivity for identity to construct an (1)-type sentence. Let us call such an expression a 'duplicate identity'. In the case of any duplicate identity, the two noun phrases flanking the verb 'to be' are tokens not only of one word or phrase type, but also of one semantic type. Hence, the triviality of any utterance of a duplicate identity.

The point of the distinction should be obvious. On the objectual analysis, any informative identity of the form of (1) is understood as making the same statement as the duplicate identity isomorphic with it; that is, a statement *a priori*, in some sense necessary, trivially analytic, and thus uninformative. It is possible to understand the statement of the political informant and yet doubt the truth of his claim. It is of course not possible to understand the isomorphic, typographically (or phonetically) identical duplicate identity and yet doubt its truth. But on the objectual account, they express the same statement. Thus the problem of informative identities stands.

It needs to be made as clear as possible at this point that this problem with informative identities as I have raised it is here generated by, and thus is displayed as a difficulty for, a particular *analysis* of identity statements. This is important to emphasise because in recent years there has been frequent discussion of informative identities as problematic for a certain kind of theory of names, of the Millian or austerely denotational variety. It is commonly believed that this sort of position, recently refurbished and popularised by Kripke, among others, along with independently acceptable semantic principles entails that standard utterances of sentences of the form of S do express the same statements or propositions as utterances of their (1)-type analogues. And this has been seen as a problem to be dealt with. But as I am presenting the problem of informative identities, it is to be understood here as a difficulty for an analysis of identity statements rather than directly for a theory of names.

For one thing, holding that proper names are not employed standardly as equivalent to definite descriptions or as tied logically to clusters of descriptions (a common explication of the thesis that names are strictly denotative, or non-connotative), is neither sufficient nor necessary for having this problem. There is a variety of ways in which a proponent of this sort of theory of names could account for a difference in information value and assertorial content between utterances of sentences of the forms of S and (1). The problem of distinguishing them arises only if the objectual analysis of identity statements also is embraced, a commitment not logically required by the general theory of names. That a non-connotative theory of names is not a necessary condition for the generation of such a problem is shown by the case of Plantinga, who in *The Nature of Necessity* held that proper names do express properties of their referents, but the properties expressed were held to be such that S and (1) should be understood as conveying the same proposition.[5] Thus the problem of informative identities sketched above need not be taken, and here is not presented, as a difficulty for a particular theory of names.

Recently, quite a few philosophers have found themselves confronting the problem of informative identities which I have claimed is generated by the objectual analysis. In many instances, it seems that they have not been completely clear on the fact that it is basically this analysis which is responsible for the problem. In any case, the common reaction has been to accept the surprising result that sentences like S, as standardly uttered, convey the same propositions as sentences like (1), and then to try to explain why it is that they seem to pre-philosophical common sense so different. It has rarely been the case that this result of the objectual analysis has been identified as such, and has been held as a good ground for rejecting it in favour of some other analysis which does not have this implication.

It must be admitted that, at least *prima facie,* informative identities do seem to create a difficulty for the objectual analysis. In the three sections which follow, I want to examine three prominent examples of recent work which might be thought to provide some means of dealing with this difficulty. These three lines of argument can be seen as providing variations on basically one approach to the problem. But each lends itself to displaying some different aspects of what I consider the weaknesses of such a position. And each is sufficiently well known to deserve comment. I believe that none of them can be taken to provide a fully plausible handling of the problem or a persuasive defence at this point of the objectual analysis.

Plantinga's regress

In his book, *The Nature of Necessity*, Plantinga presented a line of thought which might be taken as offering a possible solution to the problem I have indicated. He made the following kind of claims: S and (1) do express the same proposition, and it is necessarily true.[6] There was a discovery made with regard to that proposition, but not the one I have claimed. It was not discovered that the proposition expressed by S and (1) is true; indeed, such propositions are not discovered to be true. The discovery which the ancients made was that the sentence S does express the same proposition as (1), a necessarily true one.[7] The wording of (1) more transparently manifests the nature of the proposition expressed by it and S. It was clear to the ancients (presumably, as it is to us) what proposition (1) expresses. No 'discovery' was needed. But the particular wording or form of S so obscures *its* expression of that necessary truth that people had to discover what it in fact does express. And, of course, when they discovered *that*, they saw its truth *a priori*.

A general point which might seem to warrant Plantinga's move is that in particular cases, it may not be at all obvious what proposition is expressed by a given sentence. And we can come to discover that a sentence expresses a necessary truth. Anyone who has learned a little logic or mathematics readily will admit this. But it can be shown quite easily that Plantinga's suggestions do not employ this truth in such a way as to show with any plausibility how it can be the case that both (*a*) S expresses a necessary truth, and (*b*) it was only by a particular factual discovery that the ancients were first apprised of the truth of what is expressed by S.

First of all, it certainly seems on first thought quite implausible, if not just absurd to suggest that what was discovered by ancient star-gazers was that some one sentence, S, makes the same statement as some other sentence, (1). Whoever sat up nights staring at Hesperus, got up early to look at Phosphorus, and figured out that he was gazing at one and the same celestial body did not thereby understand for the first time the meaning of 'Hesperus is Phosphorus'. If presented with this claim at any time before his tiring vigils, he might have denied or at least doubted its truth, but there is no reason whatsoever (short of what might be dictated by an otherwise totally indefensible version of a referential theory of meaning) to maintain that apart from the final discovery he would have misunderstood it, or actually failed to understand it at all. The discovery was an astronomical, not a linguistic, one. So Plantinga's move seems from the start a misdirected one. But there is a much more serious problem with his suggestion:

His contention can be stated in the following four sentences:[8]

   (i) S expresses some proposition P.
  (ii) (1) expresses some proposition P1.
 (iii) P is 'the same as' P1.
 (iv) (iii) was discovered to be true.

Let us refer to the third sentence of this schematisation of Plantinga's suggestion in the following way:

(2)   P is P1.

Now the claim proposed can be understood as the allegation that the statement made by (2), *not* the one made by S, was discovered to be true by ancient star-gazers. But an objectual analysis of (2) reveals something quite interesting. According to this analysis, what is stated by (2) is that the reflexive relation of identity holds with regard to whatever is named by both 'P' and 'P1'. In other words, if (2) is true, then the one termed relation of identity is being truly affirmed of the referent of 'P1'. But that is precisely what is stated by the sentence:

(3)   P1 is P1.

Now, (3) is a sentence of the same form as (1), and in the same way can be seen as expressing some sort of 'funny', i.e. necessary, *a priori*, or analytic, truth. But if such a truth is expressed by (3), and (3) and (2) express the same proposition (which according to an objectual analysis they do), then (2) expresses a proposition which is true in one of these ways. It is perfectly clear that we thus have the very same problem with regard to the claim that the statement made by (2) was discovered to be true that we had with the originally problematic claim about S. This attempt to remove our problem thus generates a vicious infinite regress, in which the problem reappears at each step. It therefore constitutes no solution of the difficulty facing an objectual analysis of identity statements.

Kripke's distinctions

In his lectures entitled 'Naming and Necessity',[9] as well as in his earlier paper 'Identity and Necessity',[10] Saul Kripke presents a number of conceptual distinctions which many philosophers have thought can solve our problem. If these distinctions are acceptable, they seem to allow us to maintain both that S expresses what is expressed by (1), and that it was only by an empirical discovery that the ancients became aware of the truth of what is expressed by it. Thus, the surprising implication of an objectual analysis of identity statements would be shown to be compatible with the empirical role we know such statements often have.

First of all, Kripke makes the following distinctions, by now well known: The concepts of necessity, *a priority*, and analyticity should not be confused. Necessity is a metaphysical concept. A true statement is necessary, or necessarily true, if it is not the case that it could have been false; if, that is, the world could not have been different in the relevant respects from the way it in fact is. *A priority*, on the other hand, is an epistemological concept. A statement is true *a priori* if it can be known to be true somehow independently of experience. Kripke emphasises that the modality in this characterisation of *a priority* is *can*, not *must*. A sentence can properly be said to express an *a priori* truth even if there are circumstances or contexts in which the truth of its statement is known *a posteriori*, or experientially. And finally, the concept of analyticity is explicated by him briefly by means of the concepts of necessity and *a priority*. A statement is analytic if it is both *a priori* true and necessary.[11]

Secondly, Kripke presents the following claim concerning referential expressions: Expressions of language can be used to refer either rigidly or non-rigidly. A non-rigid designator is a referring expression which picks out a particular object by means of a property or set of properties which that object happens to have, but might not have had. In Kripke's terminology, there are possible worlds, or counterfactual situations, in which that same designating expression, by means of the same property or set of properties, refers to different objects, whichever object in each world happens to fill the conditions of its reference. The reference of a rigid designator, on the other hand, does not depend on any accidental properties of objects. A rigid designator, for example a proper name such as 'Hesperus' or 'Phosphorus', is more like a tag pinned directly onto a particular object.[12] It designates the same object in every possible world in which it designates anything at all. If its reference depends in any way on properties, it depends only on essential properties, those properties without which its referent would not exist at all. With these distinctions in hand, Kripke's position on identity can be given. In order for a sentence such as S to make a true statement, its subject and predicate nominative terms must be two designators for one object. Only on that condition will it successfully state that a certain single object bears the reflexive relation of identity to itself.[13] The question as to whether S meets that condition may be one which has to be settled empirically. So the truth of the statement made by S, as expressed in sentence S, may not be *a priori*, capable of being ascertained from the form of S alone. Indeed, it was only when the ancients discovered that 'Hesperus' and 'Phosphorus' had been used to designate the same object that they knew that S expressed a true statement.

Nevertheless, Kripke concludes from his understanding of rigid designation, if the two designators used in making that statement are rigid, the statement is a necessary truth (in a specific sense to be clarified later). In any possible world in which the object referred to in the actual world by 'Hesperus' and 'Phosphorus' exists, it bears the relation of identity to itself (its self-identity may be treated as one of its essential properties). There is thus no possible world in which Hesperus exists and is not Phosphorus. It is true that the world might have been such that these two names were used to designate two different objects, but that would not be a situation in which the object we in fact designate with those names would not be identical with itself. So the statement made by S was discovered to be true, yet it is true in some sense necessarily.[14]

If Kripke's explications of necessity, *a priority*, analyticity, and rigid designation are acceptable, then he appears to have a solution for the difficulty attending an objectual analysis of S and (1). They do express the same statement. As expressed in (1), it can be said to be analytic—known to be true *a priori*, and true necessarily. But, as Kripke has emphasised, an *a priori* statement in certain circumstances *can* be known to be true *a posteriori*, or empirically, which is the case with regard to its expression in S.[15]

At this point, we must consider carefully whether these distinctions of Kripke's can in fact be used plausibly to vindicate the objectual analysis. Let us begin by taking a second look at his distinction between rigid and non-rigid designators. It is Kripke's view that all proper names and some definite descriptions (such as 'the square root of 9') are rigid designators. Other descriptive phrases used referringly are characterised by him as non-rigid. It is one of his central philosophical theses that no rigid designator is equivalent to any non-rigid designator, or cluster of non-rigid designators. The reference of a rigid designator may be set up or fixed by means of some non-rigid designator, but their modes or referring are fundamentally different, and their referents may coincide only contingently.

It is identity statements made by the use of two rigid designators that Kripke presents as having their truth values necessarily. Such a statement, if true, asserts of some object that it is self-identical, and this cannot fail to be the case in any state of affairs (possible world) in which the object exists.[16] S and (1), both employing only names, or rigid designators, as referring expressions, thus make the (in some sense) necessarily true statement that Venus is identical with itself. And it is irrelevant to this truth conveyed by S and (1) that there are counter-factual situations conceivable in which Venus is not called both 'Hesperus' and 'Phosphorus', or even by either name. The identity statement we make by using these names is true, and true necessarily.

Turning our attention now to non-rigid designators, let us note this passage from 'Naming and Necessity':[17]

> Let 'R1' and 'R2' be two rigid designators which flank the identity sign. The [proposition] 'R1 = R2' is necessary if true. The references of 'R1' and 'R2', respectively, may well be fixed by non-rigid designators 'D1' and 'D2'. In the Hesperus and Phorphorus cases these have the form 'the heavenly body in such-and-such position in the sky in the evening (morning)'. Then although 'R1 = R2' is necessary, 'D1 = D2' may well be contingent, and this is often what leads to the erroneous view that 'R1 = R2' might have turned out otherwise.

In this passage, a distinction is drawn between identity statements made with rigid designators and those made with non-rigid designators. Concerning the latter, Kripke had said earlier in the same lectures:[18]

> . . . everyone agrees that descriptions can be used to make contingent identity statements. If it is true that the man who invented bifocals was the first postmaster general of the United States—that these were one and the same—it's

contingently true. That is, it might have been the case that one man invented
bifocals and another was the first postmaster general of the United States.

Notice carefully what is said here. Kripke gives as an example of a
contingent identity the statement made by 'the man who invented bifocals
was the first postmaster general of the United States'. He then paraphrases
this statement with the clause 'these were one and the same'. Let us ask a
simple question. To what does the plural demonstrative 'these' refer? To
the two non-rigid referring expressions? But these expressions are not
asserted to be identical. Then to two referents of these two expressions? If
so, then the statement made is not contingently true, but necessarily false. It
is impossible that *two* objects be 'one and the same' as each other. A *one*
termed relation cannot possibly hold between *two* objects. If this statement
asserts the holding of that relation in a particular case, and we are to
understand it as a true statement, then only *one* object is being talked
about. And in that case, Kripke is being at best ungrammatical in his use of
'these'. The paraphrase should be 'this is one and the same'. But if that is
what is stated, that a single object is identical with itself, then how can it be
contingently true? Are circumstances conceivable in which Benjamin
Franklin exists, yet fails to be self-identical? According to Kripke's own
understanding of identity, no. But if our modified version of Kripke's
ungrammatical paraphrase of the statement under consideration is correct,
this is what he seems to have committed himself to. And this is what an
objectual analysis of the statement would yield. The following four
sentences:

(4)   The inventor of bifocals was the first postmaster general of the
      United States.
(5)   The inventor of bifocals was the inventor of bifocals.
(6)   The first postmaster general of the United States was the first
      postmaster general of the United States.
(7)   Benjamin Franklin was Benjamin Franklin.

if they all simply make identity statements, all make the same statement
according to an objectual analysis, the statement that the object which
happens to be referred to by the referring expressions of each sentence bears
the one termed reflexive relation of identity to itself. Had the world been
different, (4)–(7) could have made different statements from the one they do
make, but the one they do in fact make—the statement most perspicuously
expressed by (7)—would still be true in any possible world in which
Benjamin Franklin existed. Thus, this is a statement whose truth value is
had in some sense not contingently, but with what Kripke calls a form of
'metaphysical necessity'. Yet, he presents (4) as a contingent statement.

In the passage from 'Naming and Necessity' we are examining, Kripke explains the contingency of (4) not by saying that Benjamin Franklin might not have been self-identical, but by saying 'it might have been the case that one man invented bifocals and another was the first postmaster general of the United States'. But according to an objectual analysis, this is not what is ruled out by the propositional content of (4). What is ruled out is Franklin's lacking self-identity.

Kripke's understanding of the content of (4) is much clearer in his earlier article 'Identity and Necessity'.[19] He calls (4) 'a contingent identity statement'. But in examining his remarks, we come to realise that there is an ambiguity in the employment of this phrase. By the expression 'identity statement' or 'statement of identity', we can refer either to a statement in which a case of identity, and that alone, is asserted to hold (its strict sense), or to a certain kind of compound or complex statement, at least one component assertion of which is one of identity (its wider sense). It is only an instance of the latter, never one of the former, which, on Kripke's views, can be contingently true. An example of the former is (7), of the latter, (4).

Kripke understands (4) as making the conjunctive statement that:[20]

... there is a man who both happened to have invented bifocals and happened to have been the first Postmaster General of the United States, and is necessarily self-identical.

(4) is thus presented as making three component assertions. Its third component is an identity statement in the strict sense, rendering it a statement of identity in the wider sense. Its first two conjuncts, neither a statement of identity in any sense, are both contingent statements, rendering the whole a contingent statement. It is only by such an analysis that (4) can be said by Kripke to be a 'contingent identity statement', which, because of the aforementioned ambiguity, is a somewhat misleading form of expression. For Kripke, no strict statement of identity, made by means of rigid designators alone, or by bound variables whose substituends can be rigid designators alone, is contingent.

Hence Kripke's ungrammaticalness in paraphrasing a contingent statement of identity as the assertion of something's being 'one and the same': on his analysis, no such statement asserts merely an identity relation, that some object is 'one and the same' as itself. His awkward use of 'these are one and the same' may reveal his understanding that *two* properties are being predicated of 'one and the same' object in any such statement, in addition to the assertion of that object's self-identity. Taken to be grammatical, of course, the expression would be incorrect; (4) does not state of any two properties or predications that they are the same. That is why we must understand Kripke's remark as being an ungrammatical, and confusing, intimation that he sees more than one thing going on in the content of an utterance of (4).

The contingency, and empirically informative content, of (4) is thus accounted for by Kripke with a Russellian analysis of the occurrences of the non-rigid designators with which it is made. This supplements, and allows for, an objectual analysis of the identity strictly stated therein, which is of course understood to be a necessary statement.

Now that we have all this out in the open, let us compare Kripke's treatment of S with his treatment of (4). If a proper name is a rigid designator and is thus not equivalent to, or synonymous with, any non-rigid designator or cluster of such designators, then no sentence having the form of S (a = b) is equivalent in meaning to a sentence having the form of (4) (The F = The G). Thus, on Kripke's analysis, S is not equivalent to

(8)   The first star to appear in the evening is the last star to disappear in the morning.

even though Hesperus is the first star to appear in the evening, and Phosphorus is the last star to disappear in the morning. According to Kripke's analysis, (8) does happen to make the statement made by S, but also makes two other statements, both contingent predictions or existence statements.

Kripke acknowledges the empirical role sentences such as (4) and (8) have in our thought, and seeks by his analysis of them as making conjunctive statements, some conjuncts of which are contingent *a posteriori* statements, to account for this. He also acknowledges the empirical role sentences such as S have but, interestingly, does little to account for this. He does say that we must first know that 'Hesperus' and 'Phosphorus' both rigidly designate the same heavenly body before we can know S to state the necessary truth that this body is self-identical. But he does not explicitly analyse S as making a conjunctive statement incorporating this semantic information.

We might be tempted at this point to supply what could appear to be lacking in Kripke's treatment of S with the following argument: If, in order for S to make a true statement, it is necessary not only that the planet Venus be self-identical, but also that both 'Hesperus' and 'Phosphorus' name this one body, then both these conditions count as truth conditions of the statement, and thus as giving the meaning of S. Consequently, it must be equivalent to

(9)   There is a heavenly body named 'Hesperus' and named 'Phosphorus' and which is necessarily self-identical.

But (9), like (4), makes a conjunctive statement two of whose conjuncts are contingent statements. Thus, it must be said to make a contingent statement as a whole. As we have seen, this is the kind of sentence Kripke understands as making a contingent identity statement. But he claims that the statement made by S is necessary.

In order to maintain a consistent position, Kripke would have to reject this possible suggestion that in order to account for the informative value of S he implies that (9) and S are equivalent. He could not block this claim of equivalence the way he would block the claim that S is equivalent to (8). This analysis does not depend on any claim of equivalence or synonymy between rigid and non-rigid designators, precluded by his general position on referring expressions. And it would not work for Kripke to claim that since S is true in any possible world in which Venus exists and is self-identical, regardless of what it is named in that world, the first conjuncts of (9) are not contained in the propositional content of S. (9) could be revised as follows:

(9') There is a heavenly body which *in the actual world* is named 'Hesperus' and is named 'Phosphorus' and which, in every possible world in which it exists, is self-identical.

It is true that what Venus is named in any counterfactual state of affairs is not part of the propositional content or truth conditions of S. But we nevertheless might be tempted to claim that what it is named in the actual world is. We have to know that both 'Hesperus' and 'Phosphorus' name the same object before we know that S states of some single object that it is self-identical.

But Kripke might claim that what is offered in (9') as part of the propositional content of S is not in fact stated by S, but is presupposed by it. The fact that one object is named both 'Hesperus' and 'Phosphorus' is an empirical presupposition of the statement made. The problem with this move is that, generalised, it would disallow the possibility of making false identity statements. And clearly such statements can be made. I can utter the sentence 'Venus is Mars' and successfully make an identity statement without the condition holding that 'Venus' and 'Mars' are both names of the same object. If they are not, then I have made a false identity statement (necessarily false, according to the objectual analysis), but an identity statement nonetheless. It *may* be a presupposition of any identity statement that the referring expressions of the sentence used to make it do in fact refer, but it cannot be a presupposition that they refer to the same thing. According to one well-known (Strawsonian) account, if the presupposition of a standardly statement-making sentence form fails to hold, that sentence fails to make a statement, true or false. If 'Hesperus' and 'Phosphorus' did not name the same object, but different ones, S would still make a statement—a false one. Whereas, if these two expressions did not refer at all, no statement would be made by S.[21] This argument for the non-equivalence of the propositional contents of S and (9′) thus does not work.

If we were to take account in *this* way of those empirical conditions which Kripke tells us we may need to discover *a posteriori* before we know S to make a necessarily true statement, we would find that, even though this analysis of S would show it to make, among other things, a strict statement of identity which is necessarily true, as a whole it would make a contingent statement. But this Kripke seems to deny, apparently holding it to make just the same statement made by (1), a strict statement of identity alone, which is necessary, *a priori*, and analytic. Fortunately, there is in fact an argument available to any proponent of the objectual analysis, similar to the one given above, on the basis of which Kripke could reject (9′) as an analysis of S.

If S and (1) make the same statement, which on the objectual analysis they do, it cannot be part of its content that 'Hesperus', a name which does not occur at all in (1), names any object. I have shown that it cannot be a presupposition for S making any identity statement at all that the two names occurring in it name the same thing. But it could be claimed that their co-designating the one object which they do name is a precondition for S making *the particular* identity statement which it does in fact make. And in that case, it would be a mistake to identify this condition as a truth condition of the statement made by S. There is an important difference between the conditions under which a certain sentence makes a particular statement, and the conditions under which that statement is true. The former, unlike the latter, will always be conditions of semantic convention.

This argument shows that (9′) and S are not equivalent in content. Thus Kripke's position can avoid the apparent inconsistency which would arise—that of holding the statement made by S to be both necessary, as equivalent to (1), and contingent, as equivalent to (9′)—if the *a posteriori*, or empirically informative, nature of the statement of S were spelled out in this way. But the question for Kripke has yet to be fully answered: How exactly does he account for the empirically informative nature of identity statements like S?

In 'Naming and Necessity', Kripke repeatedly refers to the statement made by S and to any identity statements made by the use of two different rigid designators as of *a posteriori* epistemic status. Now, according to his distinctions presented earlier, a statement which *can* in some circumstances be known *a priori* is allowably referred to simply as an *a priori* truth. Thus, since on an objectual analysis, the truth value of the statement made by S is knowable *a priori* relative to its expression in (1), it is an *a priori* truth. But since there are circumstances in which it is known only *a posteriori*—relative to its expression in S—it is also an *a posteriori* truth. Lest we think there is an inconsistency here, we should remember what we can call the context (and expression) relativity of these designations of epistemic status. The truth of the assertion that Venus is self-identical can be known either *a priori* or *a posteriori*.

But what exactly does this mean? Are there any circumstances in which we could consider the statement made by S and yet be uncertain about its truth value until we did some empirical research, until we made some *a posteriori* observations? Kripke maintains that we could be in a set of epistemic circumstances qualitatively identical, or indistinguishable, from those in which we have named one object under two sets of conditions with two names, and in those qualitatively identical circumstances, have given those two names to two different objects. It is this possibility which allows us to entertain and understand to some extent a sentence like S which contains two different names, assigned to their referents under different conditions, and not know *a priori* whether it is true. And when we learn that it is true, we have learned that we are in one possible world rather than another, so to speak. Herein lies the empirical import of S, and sentences like S.

According to this position, we are *not* informed by the statement made by S, but rather by the fact that S makes this statement. We cannot be uncertain about the truth of the statement made by S, only about what statement it does make. As in the move made by Plantinga, we have here information about what statement a sentence standardly is uttered to make. Although Kripke is more subtle and complex here than Plantinga, his account of the information content of an informative identity fails to be convincing for much the same reason. It seems obvious to prephilosophical common sense that when we utter a sentence like S, we can be *asserting* someting informative. It is not the fact *that* our sentence makes a certain statement, but *the statement itself* which is informative. If we could find no analysis of identity statements which accounts for this, then a position like Plantinga's and Kripke's might win our allegiance by default. But this, I hope to show, will not be the case.

One final point ought to be made before leaving Kripke behind. In claiming that the modal value of an identity statement is that of necessity, Kripke carefully specifies that what is meant is 'weak' necessity. A statement is said to have a modal value of strong necessity if and only if its truth value is the same in every possible world. It is weakly necessary just in case its truth value is the same in all and only those possible worlds in which any object it is about exists, and that object does not exist in every possible world. Thus it is arguable that the statement made by S may be necessarily true in this latter sense, and we may know that it is, without the empirical question of whether Hesperus or Phosphorus exists being settled for us. This raises the possibility that it is concerning the existence of some object that any true identity informs us.

But it is easy to see that this suggestion is unacceptable. It is true that we do not know *a priori* that Hesperus exists. We do not know *a priori* that Phosphorus exists. But this is not the *a posteriori* information conveyed by S.[22] We may know that Hesperus exists (presumably we do if we have a use for the name 'Hesperus' in sentences of the present tense), we may know that Phosphorus exists, and yet *still be informed* by the statement made by S. More importantly, this knowledge does not diminish the informative import of S. And this shows that no such existence statement is even part of the information conveyed by S. We do not discover *a posteriori* of any object that it is self-identical. We *do* so discover that objects exist, but it is no such statement which is made by S. It is my judgement that the whole arsenal of distinctions presented by Kripke, even though they might at many points seem to make an objectual analysis more palatable, fail to make it convincing as an analysis of the way in which identity statements ordinarily are used.

Stalnaker's admission

In his article 'Propositions',[23] Robert Stalnaker, like Plantinga and Kripke, accepts an objectual analysis of identity statements, and then tries to show how sentences such as S can thus express in some sense a necessary truth, yet be empirically informative. His comments merit inclusion here not for their novelty, but for their clarity and candour in admitting what such a defence of the objectual analysis is committed to.

Stalnaker's theory of propositions and propositional attitudes is such that doubt that a proposition is true is possible only if there are possible worlds in which that proposition is false. But, according to him, necessary truths are true in every possible world. The conclusion he draws from this about identity is that if identity statements are necessary (which in some sense they are on an objectual analysis), it must be impossible to doubt them. Now, Stalnaker recognises that we can have doubt concerning the truth value of at least some identity statements, and he has given an account of how this is possible. He first of all says[24]

> Let us consider what happens when a person comes to know that Hesperus is identical with Phosphorus after first being in doubt about it. If the possible world analysis of knowledge is right, then one ought to be able to understand this change in the person's state of knowledge as the elimination of certain

epistemically possible worlds. Initially, certain possible worlds are compatible with the subject's knowledge; that is, initially they are among the worlds which the person cannot distinguish from the actual world. Then, after the discovery, these worlds are no longer compatible with the subject's knowledge.

He then goes on to ask what possible worlds are eliminated by the discovery that S makes a true statement. They cannot be worlds in which Hesperus is distinct from Phosphorus, since, according to an objectual analysis, there are of necessity no such worlds. Stalnaker suggests that the possible worlds which are eliminated are worlds in which the sentence S is used to express a proposition other than that expressed by it in the actual world, one that is false rather than true. This would be the case with regard to any possible world in which the two names 'Hesperus' and 'Phosphorus' named not the same entity, but two different ones. And it is a contingent fact that they name what they do in fact name. Stalnaker says[25]

It is a contingent fact that the proposition expressed is necessarily true, and it is this contingent fact which astronomers discovered.

This, of course, sounds like the early Plantinga. But I shall not rehearse or augment the kind of criticisms I have already made of such a position. Something more interesting merits our attention at this point.

Stalnaker suggests that two propositions are involved in our understanding of S. First there is the contingent proposition that the sentence S expresses the proposition that a particular object, Venus, is self-identical. Then there is the necessary proposition it does express—the proposition that Venus is self-identical. He makes the following interesting admission:[26]

Now if the person, after finding out that Hesperus is identical to Phosphorus were to announce his discovery by *asserting* that Hesperus is identical to Phosphorus, what would he be saying? If his assertion is really announcing his discovery, if what he is saying is what he has just come to believe, then it is the contingent proposition he is asserting. *There is generally no point in asserting the necessary proposition*, although there is often a point in saying that what some statement says is necessarily true. (Latter emphasis mine.)

This admission actually is a crucial one. Stalnaker is making basically the same sort of move as Plantinga and Kripke, but is much clearer about an implication of it. In order to explain the empirical role or placing of the most common kind of identity statement, they both direct our attention to something *other* than the identity asserted. They both acknowledge that it is a contingent, empirical matter, knowable only *a posteriori*, that each referring expression in a sentence such as S refers to the particular object it happens to designate. Mars, rather than Venus, could have been called 'Hesperus'. Thus, it is a contingent, empirical fact that S makes the statement it does make. If, for example, Mars had been named both 'Hesperus' and 'Phosphorus', S would have made a statement different from the one it in fact makes, one about the self-identity of Mars rather than Venus. And if Mars had been called 'Hesperus', and Venus 'Phosphorus', then S again would have made an entirely different statement—it would have asserted something of *two* objects. The assignment of reference of each of the referring expressions in an identity statement is not, according to an objectual analysis, part of the content of such a statement. Yet it is to this that Plantinga, Kripke, and Stalnaker all have pointed in order to account for the empirical role these statements often have. All three philosophers have maintained that what is stated in an identity statement is that a certain case of self-identity holds in the world. And all three have understood this as being a matter of metaphysical necessity. But Stalnaker, in the passage last quoted, admits that it is not *this* which is asserted when information is conveyed by the utterance of a sentence such as S. So the question we must ask is: Why go on claiming with an objectual analysis that this is what is stated by an identity statement? What is the point of all the fancy footwork engaged in to save an objectual analysis of identity from its counter-intuitive implications? By Stalnaker's admission, the necessary statement of self-identity does not figure in the empirical role of any identity statement. Why then should any such necessary statement be accepted as the correct analysis of an identity statement of the form of S in the first place?

Paradigmatic and degenerate identities

Each of the three philosphers whose comments on identity I have discussed has accepted, or rather assumed, an objectual analysis of identity statements. In each case an attempt has been made to reconcile the result of such an analysis with the role we know these statements have in our thought and language. And in each case we have been told that it is something which is not part of the content of the identity statement which gives it its empirical placing in our thought. Stalnaker has brought out most clearly that the content an objectual analysis assigns to an identity statement is in fact *irrelevant* to our empirical concerns. No such necessary statement enlarges our empirical knowledge of the non-linguistic world. Yet identity statements seem to do this.

In The *Tractatus*, Wittgenstein wrote:[27]

Roughly speaking, to say of *two* things that they are identical is nonsense, and to say of *one* thing that it is identical with itself is to say nothing at all.

According to an objectual analysis, it is one or the other of these assertions which is made by any identity statement. Now, commentators have pointed out that Wittgenstein goes too far in this statement of admittedly some rhetorical force. To say of two things that they stand to each other in the one termed reflexive relation of identity is not to talk nonsense; it is just to utter a necessary falsehood. And why should stating the necessary truth that some one object is self-identical be equivalent to saying nothing at all? But the excesses of this assertion being recognised, we must attend to its point.

It is certainly true that at least some types of statement characterised by metaphysical necessity, true of every possible world or false of every possible world, are not empirically informative concerning the actual world. They are empirically empty. If an objectual analysis of identity statements implied that they are all members of this class of statements, it would imply that they are all empirically empty.[28] But we know this to be false. So on the basis of this unacceptable implication, we would be forced to reject the objectual analysis as unacceptable. But it should be clear that we would be wrong in trying to impugn the objectual analysis in this way. If, on the other hand, we more carefully distinguish with Kripke between strong and weak necessity, we shall see an objectual analysis as assigning identity statements concerning concrete particulars the latter modality. And it is at least arguable that statements of weak necessity, not true in every possible world, have empirically informative implications, or presuppositions, concerning the existence of some object in any world in which they are true.[29] But, of course, I have shown already that the proposition that some object exists is not part of the informative content conveyed by any identity statement. So even this possible implication of an objectual analysis is unacceptable as an account of this aspect of identity statements. What then on the objectual analysis *is* the informative content of an identity statement? Is there a sense in which Wittgenstein was right, that on this account to utter an identity statement is to say nothing at all?

As we have seen, it is, on this account, only the utterance of such a necessary statement, or the fact that the sentence uttered *makes* a necessary statement, which is empirically informative. And even this seems to be the case normally only when the subject and predicate of the sentence or clause with which it is made are tokens of two different word or phrase types. By the uttering of an *a priori* necessary statement, something is shown about language, or the concepts of a language. Nothing informative is said about the world. Yet those who accept an objectual analysis of identity understand such statements as saying something necessarily and *a priori* true about the objects they mention, while also trying to acknowledge the informative import of ordinary identities.

Is (1) informative? On the objectual analysis, it at least should inform us, if S does, that Venus stands in a certain relation. But, unlike S, (1)— understood as a duplicate identity—has none of the characteristics of an informative utterance. It seems rather to be a paradigm of the uninformative. In this notebooks, G E Moore once went so far as to write:[30]

> A sentence of the form '.......is identical with ....' *never* expresses a prop. unless the word or phrase preceding 'is identical with' is different from that which follows it.

Central to the objectual analysis is a particular account of the meaning of 'identity'. The word is supposed to denote a type of property or relation. What the property is is spelled out by the principles which are said metaphorically to 'govern' it. We are told that if the referring expressions of a sentence with which an identity statement is made successfully pick out a single object as their common referent, that statement conveys the necessarily true proposition that that object has the logically simple property of being self-identical, or of bearing the relation of identity to itself.[31] This property, or relation, standardly is taken to hold of any and every existing object. But, as David Wiggins once suggested in his early article 'Identity Statements',[32] this surely is a strange relation. If what we are speaking of is a logically simple, distinct property of synchronic self-identity, one wonders what point there is in claiming there to be such a relation, or property, at all. There certainly seems to be no empirical point in it. In fact, it looks like the emptiest sort of metaphysics. In a footnote,[33] Kripke goes so far as to call it 'the smallest reflexive relation', as if to stop one step short of fully recognising that there is no such relation at all. But it is a particular instantiation of this alleged relation that an objectual analysis sees as stated by any identity statement.

At this point, it must be asked: Is it really credible at all that S and (1) make the same statement, the statement most clearly made by (1)? Our linguistic conventions allow us to put two tokens of one word or phrase type (semantic as well as typographical or phonetic) in the same sentence, one in subject position, the other as predicate nominative, flanking the verb 'to be'. We can thus make sentences such as (1) which are syntactically impeccable. But are we thereby bound to take them seriously as identity statements?

Many traditional metaphysicians have relished the grand and vacuous

$$(x)(x = x),$$

the allegedly clear and necessary truth that all things are self-identical. We could come to see it as rather the universal generalisation of a mis-understanding. Once we come to understand the empirical placing of standard and useful identity statements, it seems to me that we should no longer be tempted to claim that they assert any discrete and logically simple property of synchronic self-identity of their objects. And once we have this new understanding, we look upon sentences like (1) with a new attitude. If it is not plausible to hold that these duplicate identities assert any such property of the objects they mention, then what do they do? It would seem, nothing.[34] But if it was only a misunderstanding of what identity statements state that led philosophers to talk of synchronic self-identity as a logically simple, essential, or necessary property of objects, or of identity as a one termed reflexive relation in which every object necessarily stands, then we have no reason to take such a property or relation to hold of any object. And then we have no such property or relation with which to interpret the metaphysicians' *a priori* generalisation. It can be seen as no more than an odd, though syntactically allowed, concatenation of signs, stating nothing.

The objectual analysis must hold sentences like (1) to offer us the paradigm for identity statements. But if I am right, it is rather sentences of the form of S or (4) which provide us with a paradigm case of identity statement. Sentences like (1), formed by reflexivity alone, are at most oddities. And the objectual analysis of identity may be at most a curiosity. I think it is primarily just because of a distinguished and hoary tradition that it continues to be assumed as the correct philosophical understanding of identity statements, in spite of its inability to account plausibly for the informative role they most often play. In the construction of formal languages, we find it useful, and indeed important for certain purposes to tack onto the predicate calculus a sign, '$=$', for 'identity', or an 'identity predicate', which is introduced and thus defined by means of some or all members of that set of laws or principles I have referred to earlier. But it is a mistake made by many adherents of an objectual analysis to think that an understanding of the identity sign in such formal languages will shed much light on the nature of identity statements made in ordinary, or natural, languages.

I should make it clear at this point that I do not think that the problem of informative identities and the few remarks just made concerning syn-chronic self-identity provide for us any sort of conclusive reason to abandon the objectual analysis. Well entrenched philosophical theses, like scientific theories and all sorts of other beliefs, do not yield so easily to difficulties which fall short of providing demonstrative disproof. And, of course, the difficulties I have raised fall far, far short of this rarely available extreme. However, the availability of a relatively attractive alternative position sometimes can itself augment the effect of a difficulty with a present position to the point of giving us what we do rightly consider good reason to abandon the old allegiance. In the next chapter, we shall examine and evaluate the account of identity statements thought by most philosophers to provide the only available alternative to an objectual analysis. This is the metalinguistic view. I hope to show that, although it is in some ways closer to the truth than an objectual analysis, it also is unacceptable as an account of identity statements. I believe that because of its problems, most philosophers have held to the objectual account in spite of its difficulties. An examination of the metalinguistic analysis will lead us to understand and appreciate better the alternative to be presented in chapter four, a position with what I believe to be sufficient attractiveness to give us good reason to abandon both the objectual and metalinguistic analyses.

2

The Metalinguistic Analysis

In this chapter, I shall examine what most philosophers have thought to be the only alternative to the objectual analysis as an explication of what is stated in an identity statement. It is an understanding of identity which has been held by such eminent logicians as Frege and Tarski.[1] This metalinguistic analysis will present identity statements as being about linguistic items, as stating a certain relation to hold between referring expressions in a language. It received its classic exposition in the writings of Frege, to which I now turn.

Frege's presentation

In the first paragraph of his well known article, 'On Sense and Reference',[2] Frege recognised the central problem with which we have been dealing in our examination of the objectual analysis. He began the article with these words:[3]

> Equality gives rise to challenging questions which are not altogether easy to answer. Is it a relation? A relation between objects, or between names or signs of objects?

After giving a brief presentation of what is roughly the same problem I have raised for the claim that identity (Frege's 'equality') is a relation holding with regard to objects—a claim of the objectual analysis—Frege went on to present the view that[4]

> What is intended to be said by a = b seems to be that the signs 'a' and 'b' designate the same thing, so that the signs themselves would be under discussion; a relation between them would be asserted. But this relation would hold between

the names or signs only in so far as they named or designated something. It would be mediated by the connection of each of the two signs with the same designated thing.

This is a very important proposal of how identity statements are to be analysed, of what exactly it is that an identity statement states. I consider this to be the only clear alternative to an objectual analysis which has been articulated and developed in the literature on the notion of identity. And it can be argued somewhat persuasively that it constitutes the substance of Frege's own considered position on identity as expressed in this well known article. But in suggesting this, I am controverting the received interpretation of his remarks.

In his book *Referring*, Leonard Linsky appears to hold that Frege rejects both the objectual analysis *and* the proposal just quoted as explications of identity.[5] It could be that Linsky is right about Frege's rejecting this latter account in favor of another one, one distinctively involving explicit talk about 'sense' and 'reference'. But it may be that his interpretation has caught the letter, rather than the spirit of Frege's subsequent remarks in 'On Sense and Reference'. I want to consider the possibility that the further distinctions Frege explicitly makes with regard to the notions of 'sense' and 'reference' can be understood as actually presenting no more than is already implicitly contained in any interesting and defensible explication of the analysis adumbrated in the above remarks.

I should make it clear at this point that it is not in any way necessary to my overall argument to establish a claim that a metalinguistic analysis of identity is elaborated within the article 'On Sense and Reference'. It is uncontroversial that Frege held this kind of analysis in his earlier writings, which I just as well could cite. But I have chosen to suggest the development of such an analysis in this later article because so doing will allow me to point out some of the subtleties of this kind of analysis which otherwise easily could be missed, and indeed have been overlooked by many critics.

After presenting the analysis of identity quoted above, Frege wrote:[6]

But this is arbitrary. Nobody can be forbidden to use any arbitrarily producible event or object as a sign for something. In that case, the sentence a = b would no longer refer to the subject matter, but only to its mode of designation; we would express no proper knowledge by its means. . . . If the sign 'a' is distinguished from the sign 'b' only as object (here by means of its shape), not as sign (i.e., not by the manner in which it designates something), the cognitive value of a = a becomes essentially equal to that of a = b, provided a = b is true. A difference can arise only if the difference between the signs corresponds to a difference in the mode of presentation of what is designated.

I have quoted at such length because this is the passage which has led most commentators to believe that Frege rejected the analysis of identity statements now under discussion in favour of another one. Let us examine these remarks by seeing how they would apply in particular to such an analysis of S.

According to what I am calling a 'metalinguistic' analysis, S states that a certain relation, that of naming the same thing, holds between the name 'Hesperus' and the name 'Phosphorus'. It does not assert the holding of a relation between two ink marks or sounds ('objects', as in the above passage), but between two *names*. An ink mark or sound 'as object' linguistically can be at most a token occurrence of a word type which, because of its particular role in a language, is, say, a name. And it is clearly between names that the identity relation here is said to hold. Moreover, Frege made it clear that the relation of naming the same thing can hold only under a particular empirical condition: the names of which that relation is predicated must have reference, and furthermore must have *the same* referent. That is to say, for the statement made by S to be true, there must be some one thing designated by both the name 'Hesperus' and the name 'Phosphorus'. So the identity relation is, according to this analysis, a two termed relation holding between actually referring expressions with a common referent.

Now Frege has claimed (and Linsky, for example, along with nearly all other commentators has agreed) that there is some sort of arbitrariness characteristic of the introduction into a language of a sign or name. He seems, further, to have suggested that this arbitrariness renders the account of identity under consideration unsatisfactory. His argument appears to be this: Any sentence of the form 'a = b' (the form of S) has a cognitive value, or informative import, different from that of any sentence of the form 'a = a' (the form of (1)). This difference must be accounted for by any satisfactory explication of ' = ', or the notion of identity. If the explication of identity under consideration would analyze any identity statement as stating merely that the relation of naming the same thing holds between whatever two marks or sounds happen to flank the marks or sounds in the verb position of the sentence with which it is made, then it would fail to account for this difference, for the following reason. If it is a fact that 'a' and 'b' are names for the same thing, it is so merely because of an arbitrary production (Frege) of these two ink marks as signs for that thing, or because of an arbitrary agreement (Linsky) to use these two marks for that same purpose. And likewise, as Searle has gone so far as to claim in his article 'Proper Names', if it is a fact that the two distinct ink marks 'a' and 'a' are both used as signs for the same thing, this also is a fact of merely arbitrary agreement.[7] Any arbitrarily producible object can be used as a sign for another object. And it is, Searle holds, merely arbitrary agreement for the sake of practical convenience that leads us to view those individual, producible objects which designate other objects as various, equivalently referring tokens of sign types. It is also possible to introduce into a language as signs or names word types different occurrences of whose tokens have different, not equivalent, reference. This often is done, for instance, in codes. Thus, to say that 'a' and 'a' (two distinct tokens of one type) designate the same thing, and to say that 'a' and 'b' (two tokens, each of a distinct type) designate the same thing is to make two statements of the same cognitive value, or kind of informative import. Different information would be conveyed by two such sentences, but the informative import would be of the same basic kind.

This is one way of putting the objection which most clearly seems to be presented by Frege. There is another form of objection which can be teased out of his remarks as well. Let us consider again the sentence S—'Hesperus is Phosphorus'. Suppose we know that 'Hesperus' is the name which has been given to the evening star, and that 'Phosphorus' is the name which has been given to the morning star. Suppose also that we do not know whether the statement made by S is true, and we are trying to find out. On the analysis under consideration, S states that the name 'Hesperus' and the name 'Phosphorus' name the same thing. Suppose finally that a friend who has a new pet dog approaches us and, noting our concern over the truth value of the statement made by S, says: 'Look here; I now name my new dog "Hesperus". I also name him "Phosphorus". Therefore, S makes a true statement. "Hesperus" and "Phosphorus" name the same thing—my dog.' What are we to do? Do we walk away glad to have the answer to our question about whether S makes a true statement? If we do not, if we do not consider our friend's pronouncements to be in any way relevant to our question, then it seems we do not consider the metalinguistic analysis of S being examined to explicate accurately what is stated by S. On this account of S, it would appear that the question whether S states a truth or a falsehood can be determined arbitrarily, as anyone chooses. If any object is or has been named 'Hesperus' and 'Phosphorus', then S makes a true statement. In that case, to determine what its truth value is, we could search the history books to see whether such a double naming with these two names ever has taken place, or, in another sense of the word, we could determine what that truth value is by ourselves dubbing something with those two names.

One conclusion we are forced to in order to circumvent this absurd possibility is that if an identity statement is an assertion about names at all, then at least the account we give of its content—of what we understand when we understand such a statement—must include something more about the names than just a recognition of their sound or physical appearance. And it is at this point that Frege attempted to provide us with something more. He drew the well known distinction between the reference of a sign, the object it designates or picks out, and its sense, 'wherein the mode of presentation (of the named object) is contained'.[8] It is quite simple to see how this distinction can be used to solve both objections developed from Frege's opening remarks.

If some name 'a' and some name 'b' have the same reference, then 'a = b' has the same truth value as 'a = a'. Yet the name 'a' and the name 'b' may have different senses. In that case, 'a = b' and 'a = a' would express different thoughts, and thus be of different cognitive value. Such is Frege's suggestion. In the case of Hesperus and Phosphorus, the irrelevance of our friend's dog naming ceremony could be clearly seen. The metalinguistic analysis of S which includes the understanding of names made explicit in the sense-reference distinction would specify that what is stated is that the name 'Hesperus' with its astronomically determined sense, and the name 'Phosphorus' with its astronomical sense refer to the same thing. The words 'Hesperus' and 'Phosphorus' as uttered by our friend have no astronomically determined senses, but a completely different sense from those about which we are concerned in our consideration of S. The sentence S as uttered by us and that sentence as uttered by him express totally different statements. The truth of one is irrelevant to the truth of the other.

It is important to realise that something like a sense-reference distinction is necessary if the metalinguistic analysis is to avoid these problems. They can be handled by it in no other plausible way. Take the irrelevance problem, for example—the canine case. Let us consider another move that readily comes to mind. As is well known, Peter Geach, among others, has argued that sentences of the form of S and (1) are incomplete in an important respect. In order properly to express a complete and determinate identity statement, the verb phrase of such a sentence must be expanded to include some general noun used to convey a covering concept for the identity, which specifies the sort of object on which the references of the two referring expressions are supposed to coincide. In the case of S and (1) as they occur in the context of astronomy, the appropriate general noun would be something like 'planet' or 'heavenly body'. In the case of the canine baptism, on the other hand, the proper general noun would be something like 'puppy', 'dog', or 'pet'. And none of these latter terms applies to the planet Venus. We are wondering whether Hesperus is the same celestial object as Phosphorus. On the metalinguistic analysis, that amounts to the question of whether 'Hesperus' and 'Phosphorus' name the same planet. Our friend's statement about a dog does not answer this question. Thus, it could be argued that when expanded into complete and perspicuous form, it becomes clear that his sentence is not uttered to make the same statement as the one about whose truth value we are wondering as we consider S. So, according to this argument, the metalinguistic analysis could avoid the problem of irrelevance just by being augmented with a thesis about the proper form of identity statements. It would not require a sense-reference distinction. And as the sense-reference distinction in the case of proper names is highly controversial to say the least, this might be thought to be a decided improvement.

But this move, unfortunately, would not provide a general solution to the problem at all. To determine the truth of S, I still could gaze heavenward, pick out any celestial object, planet, etc., and dub it both 'Hesperus' and 'Phosphorus'. And no expansion of S could eliminate this possibility. For any general noun produced to distinguish standard utterances of S from these artificial circumstances under which its utterance would be in an important sense uninformative, a case is constructible in which the irrelevant utterance employs that very same covering concept. Thus, this alternative to the introduction of a sense-reference distinction must be judged a failure as a general solution to our difficulty. That distinction, or something like it, is needed to do the job.

This talk of Frege's about sense and reference seems to be taken by Linsky to contribute to a third analysis of identity, distinct from either the objectual or metalinguistic accounts. However, it seems to be taken by quite a few other commentators to provide an apparatus to augment the objectual analysis in such a way that identity statements can be seen as asserting the one termed relation of identity to hold, but in such a way as to account for the difference between informative and uninformative forms of such statement. I am suggesting that it need not be understood in either way. It can be understood merely to be an elaboration of the analysis of identity presented at the beginning of this chapter—the metalinguistic analysis. When we review, even in rough outline, what it is for a producible mark or sound to be a sign or name in a language, we can see that Frege's first remarks require for their meaning, if they are to be at all plausible, something like what he goes on to present subsequently in his discussion of the notions of sense and reference. It is beyond the scope of this study to examine at any length the various theories of naming now vying for acceptance among philosophers, which, happily, is not required for handling the matter at hand. A few brief comments will suffice here.

The notion of sense is much clearer and less controversial in the case of definite descriptions than in the case of names. There is, of course, an ongoing battle among philosophers over whether, and if so in what sense or senses, a name can be said to have a sense as well as a reference. But in most all positions on the issue, something is affirmed of names which in some way satisfies at least one central purpose for which Frege introduced the notion of sense. Whenever we name an object, we do so in particular empirical circumstances, under particular conditions. There is some appearance of the object, or description of it, by means of which we stand in an epistemic relation to it. And whenever we learn the name of an object, we do so by means of some appearance or description of it, or other condition, by means of which it is brought to our attention. Subsequent proper uses of the name will in some way be either rooted in a knowledge of, or else dependent in some other way upon, those conditions or properties of the object in association with which it was introduced or learned as a referring expression. Philosophers have attempted to display the relation between names and those empirical conditions of the objects named in various ways. Frege said that a name has a sense in which 'the mode of presentation' of the object named is contained. Russell thought that what we in ordinary language call 'names' are really covert definite descriptions of the objects to which they refer. Searle has written of the descriptive presuppositions which underlie our uses of names. Even Kripke, whose position is actually furthest removed from those so far mentioned, talks occasionally of the descriptive information which may be needed to fix or set up the reference of a name. And finally, such causal theorists as Devitt have spoken of the perceptual conditions, causal chains, and causal networks which underlie the proper use of a name, linking it with the object to which it refers.

In each of these moves, we can see the non-arbitrary aspect of a name recognised. The mark or sound used as a name, or as a token of a name type, is tied in with much which has to do with the object named. Unless there are some circumstances or conditions of an object which allow for, or actually constitute for it, a 'mode of presentation' to human language users, it cannot be named. And a word which stands in no relation with some mode of presentation of an object is no name. So to talk of a name which is actually referring is to presuppose some link between the linguistic item which is the name and a mode of presentation of the object named. This is as true of abstract objects as it is of ordinary, non-abstract entities, though of course in such different cases the sort of link and mode of presentation involved will differ accordingly. Thus, it seems that in Frege's suggestion that identity statements be analysed as asserting the holding of a two termed relation between actually referring names, there is implicitly but necessarily present a recognition of that aspect of a name which he went on to call its 'sense'. When one ancient star-gazer said to another 'Hesperus is Phosphorus', he was asserting, according to the fully developed meta-linguistic analysis, that the name 'Hesperus', as standardly used to name a heavenly body, and the name 'Phosphorus', as so used to name a celestial object, both name the same thing.

In order to facilitate our keeping in mind this link between a name and its referent, I shall introduce here a typographical convention, for the sake of its convenience. It is a well known and normally unproblematic feature of words used as proper names that they admit of something akin to ambiguity. An utterance of the proper noun 'Hesperus' to refer to the evening star, and an utterance of 'Hesperus' to refer to a pet dog constitute the utterance of two tokens of one word type which is being used in two quite different referential capacities. Following Michael Devitt, we may say that in such a case we have one word type, but two semantic types.[9] The semantic type of a name is determined by that sort of link or 'sense' (broadly conceived) holding between the production of a token of that name and the object named. Henceforth, when I mention a name, and want to discuss its use in one of its referential capacities, that is to say when I want to denote a particular semantic type or a token of a particular semantic type, I shall employ an indexing superscript—e.g. I shall write ' "Hesperus"*' rather than merely ' "Hesperus" ' to mention the semantic type of 'Hesperus' used standardly to refer to the evening star, and, say, ' "Hesperus"**' to mention the semantic type used in some other capacity such as the name of a pet dog. Likewise, when I use the word 'name' to denote a semantic type as distinct from a word type or token, I shall superscript as 'name*'. This convention may help us to keep in mind the distinctions and commitments of a developed metalinguistic analysis.

Because of what is involved in an expression's functioning as a name in a natural language, I have suggested that the metalinguistic analysis of identity quoted from Frege at the beginning of this chapter semantically requires some such distinction as that which he went on to make with his explicit talk of sense and reference. His remarks about arbitrariness, quoted above, and the rest of the argument I have extracted from 'On Sense and Reference' *may* have been meant by him, and at least can be taken by us, to draw out and bring to light exactly what is implicit in or required by any defensible version of his own earlier account of identity. Taking that account so understood to constitute the substance of a metalinguistic analysis, we shall now move on to evaluate its adequacy as an explication of what is stated in an identity statement.

An evaluation

As we have seen, the Fregean version of a metalinguistic analysis of S presents it as asserting that the two termed relation of naming the same thing holds between 'Hesperus'* and 'Phosphorus'* under the condition that each is an actually referring expression. On this analysis, S and (1) share an existential and semantic implication, or presupposition, but clearly make two different statements. They both imply or presuppose that 'Phosphorus' has a referent, but make different assertions involving that referent. So no matter how we characterise (1), this analysis explicates S as making an *a posteriori*, empirical statement, whose truth, we can say unproblematically, was discovered by ancient star-gazers. Whoever sat up nights staring at Hesperus and finally discovered that he was staring at Phosphorus discovered that 'Hesperus'* and 'Phosphorus'* name the same thing. He discovered that these two names, which have their individual uses with regard to quite different sets of circumstances and conditions (one with regard to an appearance of the evening sky, the other with the morning sky) refer to the same heavenly body. Whereas it had been thought that there were two celestial objects which bore these two astronomical names, it was found that they named one and the same object. The estimated population of the heavens was thus reduced by one. And further, all the information previously associated with either one of these names* (excluding of course any beliefs to the effect that it was not co-referential with the other name*) was thereby associated with the other as well. All this empirical, astronomical information can thus be seen to be carried by the sentence S, in its capacity of making an astronomical identity statement.

The metalinguistic analysis thus seems to account for the empirical import of S much better than does an objectual analysis. It completely avoids the problem which attended that form of analysis. And it has thus seemed to be the correct analysis of identity statements to many philosophers. But a closer look at Frege's standard presentation of this analysis shows it to be unsuccessful as it stands. I shall describe in a bit more detail than is usual the problem many critics have recognised in the Fregean formulation, and then offer a version of the metalinguistic analysis which avoids this difficulty. I shall argue finally that although this form of analysis moves somewhat in the right direction, it fails because of a simple but powerful objection which will apply to any of its formulations.

The purpose of analysis is achieving clarity. In every successful case of linguistic analysis, the constitution or make-up of the analysandum somehow is clarified in the analysans. In the sort of analysis we are dealing with here, the analysans must be equivalent in meaning to the analysandum, or the analysis is inaccurate. But the analysans must be more perspicuous than the analysandum, or the analysis is unhelpful. And finally, the analysans must not depend for its meaning on any component or aspect of the analysandum which needs to be explained, or the analysis is impure. With these simple requirements of a successful analysis in mind, we can assess the analysis of identity statements offered by Frege.

According to Frege's version of a metalinguistic analysis, S is analysable into:

(10) The relation of naming the same thing holds between the name 'Hesperus'* and the name 'Phosphorus'*.

or

(11) The name 'Hesperus'* and the name 'Phosphorus'* name the same thing.

On the Fregean analysis, each or either of (10) and (11) is individually equivalent in meaning to S. If in fact they are so equivalent, which I temporarily shall grant for the sake of argument, then it is clear that (10) and (11) are more perspicuous than S. S invites the mistaken explication of the objectual analysis; (10) and (11) neither invite nor allow it. That is because the names 'Hesperus' and 'Phosphorus' appear merely to be used in S, whereas they clearly are mentioned in (10) and (11). It is the appearance of a purely referential use in S which is misleading, according to this analysis. The statement made by S, (10), and (11) is in large part a statement about those two names. And this is shown much more clearly by the explicit mention of them in (10) and (11) than by the apparent use of them in S. Anyone who accepts this analysis would maintain that it is this lack of clarity in the form of S, or in the surface grammar of sentences like S, which is one of the main causes of perplexity for philosophers who try to understand the notion of identity. The kind of statement made by a sentence like S cannot be read off from its form. It is a case of what Wittgenstein called language disguising thought (*Tractatus* 4.002).

The forms of (10) and (11) are neither ambiguous nor misleading. The kind of statement they make *can* be read off from their forms. It is particularly clear from the form of (10) that what is being stated is the holding of a certain relation between names. And it is particularly clear from the form of (11) that a statement is being made about these names with regard to some thing which is distinct from, yet semantically related to, them both. If (10) and (11) are equivalent to S, they can be taken to clarify it greatly. That is to say, if the analysis which has provided them is accurate, then it is also helpful.

But the question must be raised as to whether this is a pure analysis. We can consider it to be pure only if an understanding of the sentences (10) and (11) does not depend on an understanding of the problematic aspect or aspects of the sentence S. It has been claimed that S is misleading because of its form. A pure analysis of S, therefore, must result in no sentence whose form is the same as that of S, and whose expression of the statement expressed by S depends in any way upon any problematic feature of that form.

(10) and (11) clearly and perspicuously make a statement about the two names occurring in S. (10) states that the relation of naming the same thing holds between them; (11) states simply that they name the same thing. But of course this relation will hold between two names if and only if they do in fact name the same thing. So, again, we can be assured that these two sentences are equivalent, although their verbal phrasings are quite different.

The form of expression which underlies both the phrasings of (10) and (11) can be shown in the following three sentences, which jointly reveal it:

   (i) 'Hesperus'* names some object O.
   (ii) 'Phosphorus'* names some object O1.
   (iii) O is (the same as) O1.

The three conditions stated in these three sentences are the conditions which, on this analysis, are both necessary and sufficient for S to be true. They jointly constitute the state of affairs which is the holding of the relation of naming the same thing between 'Hesperus'* and 'Phosphorus'*. The Fregean analysis of S yields these three conditions as truth conditions of the statement it makes. It yields these conditions by way of either the analysans (10) or the analysans (11). If an understanding of these three sentences in no way depended on an understanding of the form of expression exemplified by S, then this analysis could be said to be a pure one. But obviously this is not the case. Consider the third sentence: 'O is (the same as) O1'. This sentence has the form of S, the form which on a metalinguistic analysis is said to be *the* problematic aspect of S. Of course, Frege has a way of understanding such a sentence. We avoid the initially attractive but inaccurate reading given this sentence by the objectual analysis when we see that it states what is stated jointly by the following three sentences:

   (iv) 'O' names some object O2.
   (v) 'O1' names some object O3.
   (vi) O2 is (the same as) O3.

But of course, once again we have a sentence of the problematic form.

The point is this: When Frege suggested that the two signs of an identity statement are asserted therein to name *the same* thing, he suggested an impure analysis of identity, an analysis whose analysans inescapably contains that which needs to be analysed (the notion of 'the same', or identity). The precise formulation of his analysis generates a vicious infinite regress, in which at each step the problematic feature needing analysis reappears.[10]

The analysis revised and assessed

The question now arises as to whether this analysis can be presented in a form which will avoid this impurity. The basic point of this metalinguistic approach is to present the manner of reference by means of which an identity statement is made as comprising part of the content of that statement. Recall from the first chapter the following sentence:

(9')   There is a heavenly body which *in the actual world* is named 'Hesperus' and named 'Phosphorus' and which, in every possible world in which it exists, is self-identical.

The statement made by this sentence presents two names as co-designative, and to this extent corresponds with the thrust of the metalinguistic analysis of S. But it also contains two features which would not be included in the metalinguistic analysis: it *states* that a certain object exists, and it predicates of that object the peculiar property, or pseudo-property, of necessary self-identity. These two features, however, can easily be removed.

Consider the following two sentences:

(12)   The object named 'Hesperus'* is also named 'Phosphorus'*.
(13)   The object named 'Phosphorus'* is also named 'Hesperus'*.

On a non-Russellian (Strawsonian) analysis of the definite descriptions occurring in the subject position, these two sentences differ in presuppositions and propositional content.[11] Unlike (9'), neither asserts the existence of any object. (12) presupposes that there is one and only one object linked with the name* 'Hesperus'* in a certain way, and asserts of that object that it also is named 'Phosphorus'*. The presupposition and assertion are reversed in (13).

I suggested earlier that in order for a sentence to express an identity statement, it must have two referring expressions, both of which actually refer. This can be understood as a presupposition of any identity statement. Thus, the identity asserted by S presupposes reference for both 'Hesperus'* and 'Phosphorus'*. Presupposing that they each have a referent, it asserts that they are co-referential. Neither (12) nor (13) alone captures the full presuppositional backing of S, but their conjunction does:

(14)   The object named 'Hesperus'* is also named 'Phosphorus'* and the object named 'Phosphorus'* is also named 'Hesperus'*.

In (14) the existential content of (9') is (on a Strawsonian analysis) relegated to a presuppositional status, and the empirically superfluous final clause is omitted. Thus, it can be seen in these respects to be an improvement over (9').

(14) could also be said to be an improvement over (10) and (11) by virtue of the fact that no identity expression such as 'the same' occurs in its formulation. It seems that in (14) the notion of identity has been analysed out. Thus the impurity affecting (10) and (11), the results of a traditionally formulated metalinguistic analysis of S, has been avoided. So it appears that it is quite easily possible to come up with a form of metalinguistic analysis free from the impurity notoriously infecting Frege's well known version.

But of course, a doubt concerning the purity of the analysis resulting in (14) and in all sentences like (14) easily can arise. It might be argued that, of necessity, if we understand (14), we understand that one object has two names. Thus our understanding the statement it makes requires our understanding counting numbers. And it can be objected that any acceptable explication of the concept of number, and clearly of what it is for one and only one object to have two particular names, will require use of the notion of identity, thereby finally rendering the analysis an impure one, though at a deeper and subtler level.

In order to defend the metalinguistic analysis at this point, a proponent would not have to deny that statements involving counting numbers can be analysed into statements involving identity expressions. If (14) is equivalent to S (an obvious condition of its acceptability as an analysis of S), then this possibility should surprise no one. The claim that would need to be argued is that we can understand statements made by the use of simple counting numbers even if we are perplexed to some extent by the form of statements of synchronic numerical identity.[12] No identity expression occurs in the surface grammar of (14). And that could be argued to be sufficient for its purity as an analysis of S. So the metalinguistic analysis is not in any way at least obviously indefensible at this point.

Another implication of this form of analysis should be examined. (14) clearly has empirical content, and is informative. In this respect, it may seem to be appropriate as an analysis of S. But we also should take a quick look at an isomorphic analysis of (1), to see how this form of explication fares as an account of its ordinarily quite different information value and status. This kind of metalinguistic analysis of (1) would yield something like:

(15)   The object named 'Phosphorus'* is named 'Phosphorus'*.

But this, on first glance, seems to have a quite different content from (1). It conveys the empirical information that a certain object has a certain name*. And no such assertion seems to be born by (1) at all. Indeed, we have been treating (1), in so far as it is merely a 'duplicate identity', as a sort of paradigm of the uninformative. Further, it is widely agreed that (1) so understood conveys some kind of necessary truth; yet the statement that a certain object happens to have a certain name surely is never necessary in any sense. Should we therefore conclude that in analysing identity statements of this form, the metalinguistic analysis goes seriously awry?

Even if nothing else could be said in defence of the metalinguistic analysis here, it might be widely conceded that the inability to explicate accurately sentences of the form of (1) need not be taken to impugn an analysis of ordinary identity statements. For as I have mentioned earlier, sentences of this form which are mere 'duplicate identities' need not be taken seriously as expressive of such statements at all. At least, admittedly, this is arguable. And even short of this position—which may well be considered by some extreme—it has been suggested in the literature on quite independent grounds that sentences of the forms of S and (1) might require different treatment, different analyses.[13] So even if the present analysis does run into trouble handling (1)-type sentences, that alone may constitute no decisive problem for it at all. It is not so implausible to hold that a difficulty explicating sentences like (1) is much less serious than a difficulty explicating those isomorphic with S, such as the objectual analysis faces.

But a somewhat stronger defence is possible here. On a Strawsonian analysis of the referring expression in subject position in (15), that sentence could not be used to make a false statement. If it has a truth value, that value will be 'true'. In this respect it is like (1) and unlike S or (14), which can make false statements. And it therefore seems to capture the kind of necessity Kripke ascribes to identity statements, the only kind of necessity defensibly ascribed to statements of synchronic identity concerning concrete, contingently existing particulars—'weak necessity'. The statement made by (1) and (15), if they are equivalent, is not simply true in every possible world. It is true in all and only those worlds in which something, a particular celestial object, is picked out by its subject term. And it seems quite reasonable to hold, with the Strawsonian analysis, that (1) and (15) are devoid of truth value, rather than false, in any other world.

Furthermore, (15) is indeed uninformative or trivial in a sense which may well be exactly that sense in which (1) has this trait. One cannot understand (15), know what statement it makes, and still be in doubt concerning its truth. Of course, it could be argued that one could know the statement (15) makes, know the truth of that statement, and yet not know of the sentence (15) that it makes a true statement. One could have this sort of doubt in this sort of circumstance. For example, one could understand

(16)   'Εσπερος Φωσφόρος εστιν

know its truth, and not knowing the English language, have no idea whether (15) makes a true or false statement. In those conditions, one would not know that (1), (15), and (16) make the same statement. But of course, that would not be a case in which one understood (15), knew what statement *it* makes, and doubted its truth. It is only this kind of doubt which is impossible in the case of (1) and (15). So in the sense in which (1) is trivial or uninformative, (15) is also. Thus, again, the metalinguistic analysis seems to hold up and to fare quite well in the face of what might at first have appeared to be a difficulty on the basis of which its rejection as an analysis of identity statements would be called for.

In claiming that Frege did reject the metalinguistic analysis, Michael Dummett has mentioned an argument on the basis of which he is said to have given it up.[14] The metalinguistic analysis purports to offer an account of the meaning of identity statements, and thereby to explicate the meaning of identity expressions, such as 'the same', 'is identical with', and so on. It claims that every identity statement asserts that whichever two referring expressions occur in the sentence with which it is made are co-referential. Dummett points to an occurrence of an identity expression which he claims this analysis completely fails to handle: the occurrence of the identity sign, '=', between two bound variables. Variables are not names, or referring expressions. Thus the metalinguistic analysis has at best nothing to say about them.

If Frege did give up the form of analysis under discussion because of this argument, he shouldn't have. The metalinguistic analysis purports to have a way of understanding the cognitive content of every identity statement. The occurrence of the sign '=' between bound variables does not *make* an identity statement, it constitutes a statement *form* for an identity statement. Assign an interpretation to all the components of this statement form, offer a substitution instance of the formula, and you will have a statement of identity. It will be this statement which a metalinguistic analysis must be able to explicate. And it will explicate it as asserting a relation to hold between the substituends of the variables. The occurrence of the identity sign between bound variables does not constitute a case for the application of the metalinguistic analysis, and so cannot be cited as a case of its failure. An understanding of the occurrence of the sign '=' will depend on an understanding of the rules according to which it is introduced into a body of symbolism, and, in so far as the formulae in which it occurs are interpreted so as to make identity statements, on an understanding of such statements, which the metalinguistic analysis offers.

There is a much more common objection against this form of analysis, which can be presented in various ways. It has seemed to many people more than odd that the metalinguistic analysis explicates every identity statement as being a statement of some fact about language. S, for example, clearly makes a statement of astronomical, not linguistic, fact. It is not about the *names* 'Hesperus' and 'Phosphorus', but is rather about the celestial object(s) they name.[15] As Quine once pointed out concerning identities asserted by sentences such as S:[16]

> . . . it is not the names that are affirmed to be identical, it is the things named.

and, again,

> . . . what are identical are the objects with themselves and not the names with one another; the names stand in the statement of identity, but it is the named objects that are identified.

But of course, Quine's remarks do not count as an objection to a metalinguistic analysis, which does not maintain that all identity statements assert the *identity* of linguistic entities. It does not confuse use and mention in this way. It does present every identity statement as making a statement about linguistic expressions, but not that sort of a statement. If it did, it would imply that every informative identity, which will of course be of the form of S, would be false. If an objection were raised along the lines of Quine's remarks, it would be based merely on a misunderstanding, and thus fail to touch this form of analysis. Furthermore, Quine's remarks seem clearly to assume an objectual analysis of identity statements as, I suppose, intuitively obvious. And any attempt to see S as asserting something about only the celestial object(s) mentioned therein must face the problem we have found to attend an objectual analysis.

But the feeling that the metalinguistic analysis goes wrong in its claim that every identity statement is a statement about language can be expressed in another way, which amounts to a very simple, and very strong objection. When we stop to think about it, it seems obvious that someone could know that Hesperus is Phosphorus without being acquainted with the two names 'Hesperus' and 'Phosphorus'. The ancient star-gazer who discovered this identity was presumably in such a situation. It seems that anyone who is acquainted with, or aware of, or in any way apprised of the existence of, the object which in fact happens to have been given the two names 'Hesperus' and 'Phosphorus' can doubt or believe or know that Hesperus *is* Phosphorus *without knowing those names*, and thus without doubting or believing or knowing anything *about* those names.[17] And if this is so, and if propositions are in any sense the objects of propositional attitudes, then the metalinguistic account of what proposition is expressed by S must be wrong. And this form of objection will of course apply to the metalinguistic analysis of any identity statement. It is a completely general criticism.

It seems clear to me that we can know an identity without knowing some particular two expressions of a language to refer to the object of our knowledge. I can know that the evening star is identical with the morning star without knowing either the names 'Hesperus' and 'Phosphorus', or the English descriptive expressions 'the evening star' and 'the morning star'. But, according to a metalinguistic analysis, my knowledge of the identity would be none other than my knowledge that some such pair of referring expressions are co-referential.

Furthermore, it seems that according to this form of analysis, the person who knows that Hesperus is Phosphorus has a completely different piece of knowledge from the person who knows that the evening star is identical with the morning star. And this is certainly counter-intuitive. Surely a single informative identity statement can be expressed in different sentences composed of different pairs of referring expressions.

Finally, it is interesting to note that the philosophers who have propounded the metalinguistic analysis have displayed its results with regard to sentences of the form of S, made with two names, but have failed to be as clear about its handling of sentences of the form (4), (5) and (6)—sentences whose subjects and predicates are both descriptive phrases rather than names. Whatever initial attractiveness there might be in analysing an identity stated with the use of names to be an assertion that those two linguistic items are co-referential, there is much less so, if any at all, in such a claim about an identity stated by the use of descriptive phrases. Had there been no English language, and had the phrases 'the first postmaster general' and 'the inventor of bi-focals' thereby not existed as the descriptive phrases which they in fact happen to be, it nevertheless could have been the case that the first postmaster general was identical with the inventor of bi-focals. It would seem much more reasonable to analyse any such statements as asserting that some one object has two properties rather than that it is picked out by two co-referential expressions.

However this type of objection is put, I believe it is as decisive as one could want against the metalinguistic analysis. And I think that it is as a result of such an objection that most philosophers now find it unacceptable. An awareness of this kind of problem, combined with a belief that this account and the objectual analysis are the only alternatives there are for explicating identity statements, has driven so many of them to hold and defend the latter in spite of its difficulties and metaphysical entanglements. In the next chapter, I shall explore briefly what lies behind this belief that we have only two options available for a philosophical account of identity statements. And in chapter four, I shall develop a new alternative analysis of such statements, which has only been hinted at by a few recent writers. It is in some ways a move in the spirit, but certainly not according to the letter, of the metalinguistic analysis. And it avoids the objection on which that analysis foundered. But what is more important is that it results from a new way of approaching a philosophical understanding of identity statements.

3

The Dilemma

At this point we have taken a look at the two prominent analyses of identity statements, one or the other of which almost all philosophers hold. I have indicated difficulties attending each, and on that basis have withheld acceptance of either. To anyone familiar with the literature, my failure to endorse either anlysis may seem puzzling. Although to my knowledge no one has stated it explicitly, it seems to have been believed very widely by writers on the topic that these two analyses are, in some form or other, the only alternatives available as a philosophical account of identity statements. If this were true, we would be faced with a dilemma. One of the two analyses would have to be accepted in spite of its difficulties. In this chapter I want to suggest that philosophers indeed have found themselves faced with this dilemma because of one major assumption and a method of analysis they have brought to bear in their attempt to understand identity statements. This assumption, method, and resulting dilemma have functioned as a sort of framework of understanding which has determined to a significant extent the dynamics of recent discussions of identity statements, and actually has kept most philosophers from attaining a clear understanding of them. The framework has caused them to think that the discovery of a problem attending one of these two analyses is itself, all else being equal, reason to accept the other.

I want to suggest that we can achieve a perspicuous philosophical understanding of identity statements only by dismantling that framework. By rejecting its major assumption and reversing its method of analysis we shall be able to escape the dilemma and construct a new account of identity statements.

A framework of thought

First of all, let us look at the usual *modus operandi* of philosophers when approaching our topic. It has been the common procedure to begin with an understanding of the *notion* of identity and then bring this to bear on an analysis of identity *statements*. Toward the end of chapter one I have suggested that this lies behind the objectual analysis. What is important to realise is that it also undergirds the metalinguistic position. Many philosophers have understood the notion of identity from the perspective of the sign '=', or an identity predicate, as it occurs in formal systems. Identity is taken to be a relation governed by the principles of reflexivity, symmetry, transitivity, and Leibniz's Law.[1] This is the common ground of the objectual and metalinguistic analyses. They differ only in that the former sees that relation as one termed, holding only between an object and itself, whereas the latter presents it as the two termed relation of co-referentiality. In either case, all the formal principles are satisfied.

So when it comes to giving an account of identity statements, most philosophers think they know what identity is. It thus makes sense that they understand such statements as asserting the identity relation to hold or be instantiated in particular cases. What could be more obvious? This is what a statement of identity is. It informs us of a particular case of self-identity or co-referentiality between referring expressions. So it has been held.

Before going on, I want to say a bit more about synchronic self-identity. We might be unfair to those who hold an objectual analysis if we attributed to all of them the position that the English 'self-identity' denotes a simple property or universal capable of multiple instantiation. Subscription to this analysis does not in itself involve this specific commitment. John Woods, for example, has said that '. . . self-identity is, in one clear sense, an utterly general property, true of everything there is . . .',[2] but has added that:[3]

> It cannot be denied that self-identity is a funny kind of property. Certainly it is not a *universal* since it is not instantiable by more than one individual. It is not, that is to say, a property such that every individual has it, even though it is true that every individual is self-identical. . . . Every individual has *its* self-identity, and every case of self-identity is unique to just one individual.

In his recent book *Identity and Essence*, Baruch Brody has given the following line of reasoning:[4]

> The existence of properties is postulated by the realist account of truth; sentences are true just because certain objects have certain properties. Now suppose it is true that $a = a$ but false that $c = a$. What property is it which a has but which c lacks that makes the first claim true and the second false? It cannot be the general property of self-identity, since both a and c have that property. It must, I submit, be the property of-being-identical-with-a.

Woods denies that there is a property of self-identity which is, like ordinary properties, multiply instantiable. He holds only that any identity statement asserts of the referent of its referring expressions that it has its own self-identity. Thus 'self-identity' does not denote a single property, but rather acts as a predicate *form*, whose application always must be supplemented contextually so that what is predicated is 'identity-with-a' or 'identity-with-b', where a and b are the objects to which self-identity is ascribed. Brody also draws this distinction, although he accepts both understandings of 'self-identity'.

It seems to me utterly vacuous to say that, for example, Venus has a logically simple, distinct property of being identical with Venus.[5] And surely it is a strain on pre-philosophical common sense, if not also on the imagination, to hold that there are all these uniquely instantiable basic properties at least equinumerous with the existent property bearers in the universe, whose exemplifications pop into and out of existence only with the appearance and disappearance of the subjects they characterise. It is puzzling enough just to talk of a logically simple property which in principle fails to admit of multiple instantiation. And I know of no one who has dispelled convincingly any of this puzzlement.[6] In the book just mentioned, Brody thinks he has a straightforward way of alleviating some of the discomfort that attends the claim that there is such a property. But his remarks are in fact irrelevant to the problem. He presents for our consideration the phrase 'being the first person to walk on the moon' which neither he nor anyone else would hesitate to understand as denoting a property, 'even though the property in question can only be had by one object'.[7] But the fact that we do not scruple at this kind of property has nothing to do with the kind of uneasiness we may feel about synchronic self-identity. There is a modality mix-up here. The moon walking property, like any first, last, or superlative property, strictly taken, can be had by only one individual in the actual world, or within the bounds of any single possible world. But unlike any of the myriad alleged properties of self-identity, it admits of instantiation by different objects in different possible worlds. Some other person could have been first to walk on the moon. But it is impossible that some other object could have been identical with Venus.

So there are difficulties enough with swallowing this understanding of self-identity. But as far as I am concerned, the construal of self-identity as a universal which *is* multiply instantiable, a position rejected by Woods but also accepted by Brody, is even less intelligible. What in the world of metaphysical import does everything existing have in common with everything else existing aside from the mere fact of its existence? And identity, if it is anything, is not existence. The point I want to make here is this. On an objectual analysis of identity statements, identity is understood as a relation which most accurately is characterised as 'self-identity', as construed in at least one, but not necessarily both, of the above ways.

Neither of these explications of self-identity strikes me as displaying to us a property or type of property which we have any reason to ascribe to any object at all. And this contributes to our dilemma.

When philosophers have sought to understand identity statements thinking they already understood identity, they have begun their analysis with a property or relation in hand which they then took these statements to attribute to objects in the world. And this has been either self-identity or co-referentiality. But as I hope to have indicated in chapters one and two, as well as in the remarks above, neither alternative is without difficulties. Neither is convincing. I believe that it has been a wrong method to try to understand identity first and then to try to give an account of identity statements based on that. I want to suggest that we can attain some clarity and some plausible results in this area only by first looking at identity statements and how they are used in natural languages. Then, on *this* basis, we may be able to arrive at a plausible understanding of the *notion* of synchronic identity. It is this reversal of method which the next chapter will exemplify. The dismantling of the framework of understanding which has underlain recent thought about identity and identity statements will be half accomplished when we make this simple switch in method.

But the framework and its resulting dilemma are comprised not just by this method of analysis. Its other component is a major assumption about identity statements. Like the appropriateness of the method of analysis just rejected, its truth has seemed so obvious to philosophers that it has gone almost entirely unmentioned, and certainly unargued, in the literature. This is the assumption that there can be an answer to the question: Exactly what does an identity statement state? Adherents of both the objectual and metalinguistic analyses have assumed that this is a proper question to ask, and that an answer to it can be given. Actually, this can be understood as a two-layered assumption. On a general level, it is assumed that there is something all identity statements state, namely that a certain property or kind of property is instantiated, or that a certain relation holds. And of course the choice we have is between self-identity and co-referentiality. On a different level, it is assumed that any particular, individual identity statement has a determinate content of assertion. Realising that identity statements can be informative, most philosophers thus have assumed that they have determinate cognitive content.

If we assume that it is proper to ask either the general or the particular question, we have trouble finding a satisfactory answer. For, as I have pointed out, the only clear answers in the literature are provided by the objectual and metalinguistic analyses. And neither of them is plausible. So if we must answer these questions, and these are our only alternatives available as answers, we are faced with a dilemma. But, again, I believe that we are no more stuck with this assumption than with the method of analysis which has been so widely practised. In the next chapter I hope to show that a satisfactory account of the informative import of identity statements can be given without accepting this assumption at all. There I shall try to arrive at an account of how they carry information without presenting them as having any particular, determinate content.

The framework's effect

So this is the method of analysis and the major assumption which I have claimed constitute a framework of understanding within which most all discussions of identity statements have taken place. The most salient feature of this framework is, as I have indicated, its crowning dilemma of choice between the objectual and metalinguistic analyses as our only options for a philosophical account of identity and identity statements. At this point, I would like to give a couple of examples of recent well known discussions in which I believe the framework to have been operative, and to have had something of a distorting effect. I choose two examples which will pick up on some of the argument of the first two chapters. First, a word about Frege scholarship.

In the last chapter, I suggested the possibility of a heretical interpretation of Frege's position on identity in the famous article 'On Sense and Reference'. As I mentioned there, in his earlier writings he clearly propounded the metalinguistic analysis of identity statements. However, the opening remarks of 'On Sense and Reference' have sounded to most readers like a retraction of that position. Indeed, as I have indicated, Frege does show there that the metalinguistic analysis cannot be understood in a certain way if it is to be of any plausibility at all. But most commentators have taken his remarks to signal a complete rejection of the account. They see his subsequent development of the distinction between the sense and the reference of a referring expression to be the elaboration of an apparatus which allows the objectual analysis to be maintained by accounting for the difference between an informative and an uninformative form of identity statement. Thus, he is seen as having discovered a problem with the metalinguistic analysis, and thereby having turned to embrace the objectual one. Now, it is true that a few commentators at times seem to talk as if he had constructed a new analysis, a third alternative distinct from these other two. But on closer inspection, I believe it can be seen that they really hold his position to be a dressed up and augmented objectual account.

It seems to me that at least to some extent commentators have been so quick to hold this reading of Frege because they have considered a simplistic, crude version of the metalinguistic analysis, and the objectual account to be really the only alternatives available. A problem seen in one would then surely be a reason for holding the other. So they have thought. I dissent from the accepted reading in two ways. First, as indicated already, I do not see the passage in question as presenting a decisive criticism or rejection of the metalinguistic approach. And secondly, my perspective on identity statements is not such that I would see this sort of rejection as necessarily signalling an acceptance of the objectual alternative. As I have made clear, I do not share the framework of thought in which these accounts are the only options. I believe in fact that Frege's criticism of a superficial form of the metalinguistic analysis moved him into a position which to some extent anticipated the analysis I shall propound in the next chapter as the correct philosophical account of identity statements. That this is so is indicated indirectly by the fact that my own account derives its impetus from Strawson, who in turn shows the influence of Frege in many relevant ways. But within the bounds of the article in question, Frege can be understood as providing essential components for a defensible form of metalinguistic analysis.

I have brought up this bit of Frege scholarship only for a modest purpose—to point out a way in which the pervasive framework I have alleged to affect discussions of identity has in a concrete instance influenced what philosophers have said. Practically the only commentators who have refrained from attributing to Frege a move to the objectual analysis in this article have held only that either we cannot tell from the article what position he is taking, or he himself was not clear about it.[8] No one has suggested, as I have, that he can be understood as continuing to hold a metalinguistic account. But more illustrative of my point here, no one has made it clear that even if he did reject it, that in itself would not alone indicate his acceptance of the objectual analysis. Nearly everyone has talked as if they are both mutually exclusive *and* jointly exhaustive of the field of possible analyses of identity statements. The latter, I hope to show by the results of the next chapter, they are not.

Let us take a look now at another well known recent discussion of identity whose structure is determined by the framework in question. It is an argument given in two places by Saul Kripke. A look at it should be interesting in more than one way. Speaking of the metalinguistic analysis, Kripke has said:[9]

If anyone ever inclines to this particular account of identity, let's suppose we gave him his account. Suppose identity *were* a relation in English between names. I shall introduce an artificial relation called schmidentity (not a word of English) which I stipulate to hold only between an object and itself. Now then the question whether Cicero is schmidentical with Tully can arise, and if it does arise the same problems will hold for this statement as were thought in the case of the original identity statement to give the belief that this was a relation between the names. If anyone thinks about this seriously, I think he will see that therefore probably his original account of identity was not necessary, and probably not possible, for the problems it was originally meant to solve, and that therefore it should be dropped, and identity should just be taken to be the relation between a thing and itself. This sort of device can be used for a number of philosophical problems.

In another place he has given the following general account of his strategy using 'schmidentity':[10]

> I propose the following test for any alleged counter-example to a linguistic proposal: If someone alleges that a certain linguistic phenomenon in English is a counter-example to a given analysis, consider a hypothetical language which (as much as possible) is like English except that the analysis is *stipulated* to be correct. Imagine such a hypothetical language introduced into a community and spoken by it. If the phenomenon in question would still arise in a community that spoke such a hypothetical language (which may not be English), then the fact that it arises in English cannot disprove the hypothesis that the analysis is correct for English.

It seems that Kripke holds the following assessment of the objectual and metalinguistic analyses: The former is somehow *prima facie* more plausible, but it seems to be attended by a problem, the difficulty, or 'counter-example' of the informative import of most ordinary identity statements. It is on the basis of this problem that some people have turned to a metalinguistic analysis. But this is an unnecessary move. For stipulate that there is such a one termed reflexive relation as the objectual analysis takes identity to be. Call it 'schmidentity'. The same phenomenon of informative import would arise in the case of schmidentity statements as is present in the case of normal identity statements. This would be so because the question could arise as to whether Cicero and Tully, or Hesperus and Phosphorus, are schmidentical. And where there is a real question, there can be an informative statement answering it.

So we could have informative schmidentity statements. But the possibility of adverting to a metalinguistic analysis to account for that information would be cut off by stipulation. What does this show? It shows, according to Kripke, that identity statements could be informative even though identity is a one termed reflexive relation, holding only between an object and itself. Thus, it is not possible to use the phenomenon of informativeness as a basis for rejecting the objectual analysis, and instead propounding the metalinguistic view. Kripke evidently feels that this line of reasoning shows the latter to be unneccessary. And it is really the only argument he gives for rejecting it and maintaining the objectual account instead.

There are two things I want to say about this argument. I have introduced it here because it exemplifies something quite simple about the dynamics involved in almost any dispute over what the correct account of identity statements is. And this is what I mainly want to point out. But first, a quick probe at the argument itself.

It is a crucial premise in Kripke's argument that 'the question whether Cicero is schmidentical with Tully can arise'. For if no such question can arise, no statement that Cicero and Tully *are* schmidentical can be informative. So let us see how such a question could arise.

Assuming that the names 'Cicero' and 'Tully' are actually referring expressions, either Cicero and Tully are two objects, or there is one entity with both names. Now suppose first that we are dealing with two objects. Can the question arise as to whether they are schmidentical? Only if two objects can stand in this relation to each other. But this is precluded by the stipulation that schmidentity holds only between an object and itself. Thus, the question could not arise.

But suppose that we are dealing with only one object. Can the question then arise? Well, either all objects are schmidentical, or only some are. If all objects stand in this relation, there can be no real question needing an answer as to whether some one particular object does. If, on the other hand, not all objects are schmidentical, it would seem that the question *could* arise. But here we face two problems. If schmidentity is such that it does not hold of every object, then it is so different from identity, as understood in the objectual analysis and thus presumably by Kripke, that no conclusion we reach concerning it is necessarily applicable to our understanding of identity. So the argument as a whole would seem to break down. And even setting this aside, we can ask what it is about schmidentity which would allow us to answer the question of whether it characterises some particular object. Is it an individual, discrete empirical property? If it is anything like identity, presumably not. But if not, how is its presence or absence detected? Without an answer to *this* question, we do not know how to answer the original one. And is a question whose answer we in principle seem to have no way of discovering a real question at all? The force of this latter query, it should be noted, is in no way dependent on any obviously objectionable form of verificationism and is, I think, substantial.

Now, certainly, a question *can* arise as to whether 'Cicero' and 'Tully' name one or two objects in some context of their use. But this, by stipulation, is not the question of whether Cicero is schmidentical with Tully. Likewise with the question as to whether an object having the two names exists; it can arise as a real question, but it is not the schmidentity question. It seems to me that we must conclude that no such question as the latter can arise at all. Thus Kripke's argument breaks down around this one premise, and so must be judged unsuccessful. He does not show the compatibility of the informativeness of identity statements with the account of their content provided by the objectual analysis. And so he does not relieve us of the need to consider some other analysis. If he had been successful here, the account of identity statements to be proposed in the next chapter might be judged unnecessary, or at least might be assimilated in some way to the objectual analysis, as mere icing on that philosophical cake. I point out the failure of Kripke's argument to underscore the need for a new analysis which is independent of the objectual account.

But the argument has been introduced here actually to make another, much simpler, point. Kripke's remarks exemplify the operation of the framework of thought which needs to be rejected. He treats the objectual and metalinguistic analyses as if they are our only options. His argument employing 'schmidentity' is meant to impugn the latter and *thereby* to reconcile us to the former. Or more accurately, it is intended to eliminate a reason for adverting to the latter and allow us to maintain the former. What we must be quite clear about is that any difficulty with the objectual analysis does not *in itself* serve as reason for holding the metalinguistic account, only for adopting *some* other analysis. And the converse holds as well. Whether or not they would actually espouse the elements of the distorting framework, recent writers like Kripke certainly have acted as if they did in their treatment of the objectual and metalinguistic analyses as the only alternatives for a philosophical account of identity.

4

A Functional Analysis

We are trying to understand identity statements. Or, rather, we are trying to give an account of the understanding of identity statements we have when we are not doing philosophy. Our concern is specifically the cognitive content, or informative import of such statements as ordinarily used. In the previous chapters I have examined the two accounts one or the other of which has been held by almost every philosopher who has commented on identity. The difficulties which attend them seem to render them unacceptable as analyses of identity statements. In this chapter, I shall sketch out an account which I believe to capture accurately their meaning. It is an alternative analysis only hinted at by a few philosophers in recent years, none of whom have developed it in any detail. It has not yet even been recognised as a distinct philosophical view competing with the others. So it may be considered a new account of identity statements.

Predications and identities

I think the metalinguistic analysis comes a lot closer than the objectual one to giving an accurate account of what identity statements as they ordinarily are used communicate. It represents an improvement over the latter in two respects. First, it does not treat identity as a distinct metaphysical property or relation exemplified by every existing object. And, more importantly, it stresses the fact that any utterance of an identity statement presents us with two ways of talking as ways of talking about only one object, or with two referential expressions as co-referential. And we shall see that something somewhat akin to this recognition will play a central role in an acceptable account of such statements.

But, as I have argued, the metalinguistic analysis makes the mistake of claiming that an identity statement *asserts that* the two referential expressions with which it is made are co-referential. We have seen that this is unacceptable as an explication of its content. I would like to suggest that it and the objectual analysis go wrong for a common reason. They both treat identity statements as predications, and so assume that for any such statement, a determinate, single answer can be given to the question: What does it state? It is assumed that, since identity statements often are informative, an answer can be given to the question, of exactly *what* do they inform us? Peter Strawson has made the following suggestive counter-proposal:[1]

> In the case of any ordinary predicative proposition, we can give a general account, valid for all audiences, of *what* anyone who is informed by that proposition is informed of; whereas in the case of an identity-statement, it does not seem that we can do this. But this does not mean that in the case of a given identity-statement we cannot give a general account, valid for all audiences, of *how* anyone who is informed by that proposition is informed. To be able to do this is to be able to say in what the general informativeness of that proposition consists.

In a predication, some subject is introduced—what the statement is 'about'—and a property is attributed to that subject. The problem we have found with treating identities as predications is that if they are 'about' the referents of the referring terms of the sentences with which they are made, then either they are trivial and uninformative, or inform us at best that a certain object exists. But they seem to be neither trivial nor equivalent to existential assertions. So what else can they possibly be about? The referring expressions themselves? But this is the claim of the metalinguistic analysis, which we have seen to be mistaken. Although realising that there are problems with either alternative, most philosophers have thought that these were their only options for explicating the informativeness of identity statements. So they have remained content with choosing their poison, and pretending, with patently implausible claims, to provide an antidote.

There is a simple way out of this dilemma. We can cease to treat identity statements as predications.[2] And we can cease to ask exactly what they state, a perfectly proper question for any kind or class of predication, instead seeking to determine what they *do* and *how* they do it. This is the direction I shall take in this chapter. I shall try to account for the informative import of identity statements as they are used in ordinary language by offering an account of them in terms of their cognitive *function*. In an important sense, I am taking here a Wittgensteinian turn. The resulting analysis will be referred to as 'a functional analysis' of identity statements.

We should get fairly clear, before going on, about what kind of sentence can be used to make an identity statement. So far we have merely relied on what most philosophers have taken to be examples of sentences para-

digmatically serving to make such a statement. But some general specifications can be given. An identity statement is made by any sentence, or,
more exactly, by any standard use of a sentence, of the syntactic form noun
phrase—verb—noun phrase, where the verb is the verb 'to be', standing
alone, or augmented by identity expressions ('the same as', 'identical with',
'no different from', 'not distinct from', etc.) and the noun phrases are
actually referring expressions.[3] It is my opinion that the noun phrases must
be tokens of two different semantic types, but I do not explicitly include this
as a restriction for a simple reason. I do not want to complicate matters here
by having to argue that any violation of such a specification would result in
no identity being stated at all, rather than merely in the statement of a
trivial identity. But as I have indicated earlier, this is my own position.[4]

Philosophers at least since the time of Plato have distinguished between
different functions of the verb 'to be'. In English, it is used in predications,
existential assertions, to indicate class inclusion, and as an auxiliary verb. It
is also used in the making of identity statements. It is a mistake to assimilate
this distinct function to one of the others. Specifically, the 'is' of identity
should not be confused with the 'is' of predication. E J Lemmon has
provided two simple tests for distinguishing this use of the verb 'to be':[5]

> Aids towards recognizing the 'is' of identity are: (a) can 'is' be replaced by 'is the
> same object as'?—if so, 'is' is 'is' of identity, if not, not; (b) can the phrases
> flanking 'is' on both sides be reversed preserving approximately the same
> sense?—if so, 'is' is 'is' of identity, if not, not.

His first test is incorporated into my account of the form of sentences which
can be used to state identities. The rationale for his second test will become
clear later.

The two noun phrases of an identity statement must be referential
expressions which actually refer. Included in this class will be at least names
and referentially used definite descriptions. On a Russellian analysis,
descriptions attributively used (their semantically standard use) which
flank the verb 'to be' will contribute only to the making of a statement
whose overall logical form is not that of an identity statement. On a
Strawsonian analysis, they can figure in an identity assertion so long as they
actually refer, or, to be terminologically more accurate, so long as they in
fact have denotation and are used as such. My restrictions on the noun
phrases are fairly liberal, compared to those specified by some writers.[6] A
sentence whose form meets these requirements can be used to make an
identity statement, and none other can.

To see how definite descriptions can be used in the making of an identity
statement, let us look again at sentence (4), 'The inventor of bifocals was
the first postmaster general of the United States.' (4) is used to make an

identity statement when and only when Lemmon's two tests are satisfied. First, it must be possible to augment the verb of (4) with an identity expression such as 'the same person as', or even to rearrange the components of the sentence, while augmenting the verb, in such a form as 'The inventor of bifocals and the first postmaster general of the United States were one and the same person', without thereby altering the sense of the sentence, or changing the statement made. Secondly, it must be possible to reverse the two descriptions and yet still make the same statement.

It is the necessity of satisfying this second test which will tell us how the noun phrases in (4) are being used and what kind of statement it is making when it is used to state an identity. Clearly, the reversal procedure would not be possible *salva significatione* if (4) were used to attribute the property conveyed by its predicate phrase to the object denoted or referred to by its subject phrase. The possibility of this reversal shows that what Strawson has called the 'presumption', and Michael Lockwood the 'assumption', of knowledge and of ignorance on the part of his audience made by any speaker intending to make an informative identity statement by his utterance of a sentence like (4) in a standard conversational context is different from what it would be if he were attempting to make an ordinary, informative predication by its utterance. To be more specific, in any situation in which a speaker attempts to make an informative statement of any sort, he makes certain assumptions about the epistemic state of his audience. He makes certain assumptions concerning what they do, and what they do not, know. And these are of two types, linguistic and extra-linguistic. The linguistic assumptions are merely that his audience is familiar with the meanings of his words in a definitional or functional sense.[7] That is, they know or have command of any linguistic conventions on which his utterance depends. The extra-linguistic assumptions are characterised by Lockwood as follows:[8]

> The knowledge assumed is that which is required if the hearer is to identify what is being referred to by such referential terms as the sentence contains. It will be assumed that he is acquainted, in some sense, with the object or objects referred to and possesses sufficient knowledge of their attributes or relations to be able to tell from such descriptive or demonstrative content as the referential terms embody that it is these individual(s) that the speaker has in mind. What it will standardly be assumed that the hearer either does not know, or can at least be usefully reminded of, is that the individual or individuals in question possess whatever attributes or relations are being ascribed to them by the speaker as the main substance of his assertion.

The extra-linguistic assumptions are different for identity statements and predications.

When (4) is uttered to make an identity statement, it ordinarily is assumed that the audience knows that someone invented bifocals, and that someone was the first postmaster general. When it is uttered to make a predication, only the former assumption is made. The latter becomes part of the content of the proposition asserted. And in the case of the identity statement, it is further assumed that, whatever beliefs are held about the person singled out by each of these descriptive phrases, it is not believed that he had the property conveyed by the other description. Simply put, the assumption of ignorance is that the audience does not know, or can usefully be reminded, that one person both invented bifocals and served as the first postmaster general of this country. Yet the identity statement is not a conjunctive predication. Used to state an identity, (4) does not assert of a particular person that he had these two properties. It does not, for example, make the same statement as the sentence—'Ben Franklin both invented bifocals and served as the first postmaster general.' It might more accurately be called a 'metapredicative statement'. But only if that is not taken to imply that it predicates something of predications. (4) states neither that Ben Franklin had two particular properties, nor that those two properties are co-instantiated, nor that predications of both those properties are ascriptions to one and only one bearer of properties. In its role as conveying an identity statement, it has a different function.

The epistemic function of identity statements

An informative identity statement has the epistemic function of collating or connecting different bits and bodies of information about the world. This is its cognitive role. If I accept the identity statement conveyed by (4) as a true statement, I thereby collate, or bring together, whatever information (however minimal or extensive) I may have about whoever invented bifocals, or about the particular person whom I believe to have invented them, and whatever information I likewise may have pertaining to the first postmaster general, or the individual I believe to have had that distinction, as information about one person. Whereas it was possible that two different people had those two different properties, one apiece, and whatever other properties might be in certain ways associated with each of them, the utterance of (4) as an identity statement collates both sets of expressed and associated properties as properties all had by one person.[9] In an article entitled 'Identity and Reference', A J Ayer has written:[10]

> The cash value of the statement of identity is contained in the contingent proposition that two different states of affairs are related to one another in a way that is sufficient to make them elements in the history of one and the same object.

This is roughly right in its basic insight, but is misleading as Ayer has put it. (4) does not, when used to make an identity statement, serve to predicate of some object, identifyingly referred to as a subject of predication, a pair of determinate, or completely specified, sets of properties. To avoid this implication, I have been careful to employ in my own remarks above such indeterminate phrases as 'whatever information' and 'whatever properties'. I shall discuss the modality of an identity statement's 'cash value' in the next chapter.

In order to elucidate further the difference between a predication and an identity statement, we can borrow some vivid imagery from Strawson and Lockwood, only the former of whom uses it to the same purpose. Let us turn first to Strawson, who provides two 'models' for the acquisition of knowledge, in his little, and little known, book, *Subject and Predicate in Logic and Grammar*.[11] These models he also refers to as 'pictures'.

Strawson first has us picture to ourselves a sort of knowledge-map (or more cautiously, 'belief-map'). On this map are many dots, each representing what he calls a 'cluster of identifying knowledge'. Simply put, they each represent some propertied individual about whom we have some knowledge. The rest of the map is filled out in the following way: Any proper name by which we refer to an object is written on the map adjacent to the dot which represents its bearer. From each dot radiate lines bearing predicate expressions. These represent all the propositions we are able to affirm of each object falling within the scope of our knowledge. Lines representing relational propositions join the dots standing for their relata. Other lines, representing non-relational propositions, are joined to a dot at only one end, and so forth.

This knowledge-map picture can be used to represent the various ways in which new information is added to our stock of knowledge. Let us consider someone with such a map who receives some new information. It will be communicated to him by the utterance of a sentence containing some expression by means of which he is able to identify the cluster of knowledge to which the statement is directly relevant. Strawson describes some different possible alterations in his knowledge-map in the following way:[12]

> When the statement to which he is audience is an ordinary relational statement, he draws a further line between two dots. When it is a statement ascribing some non-relational property ... to one of his items, he draws a further line of the kind which terminates in a dot at only one end. But when it is an identity-statement ... he adds no further lines. He has at least enough lines already ... and certainly one too many dots. So what he does is eliminate one dot of two, at the same time transferring to the remaining one of the two all those lines and names which attach to the eliminated dot and are not already exactly reproduced at the surviving dot.

He then goes on to draw his general conclusion from this pictorial representation, worth quoting in full:[13]

> And this gives us a general picture, valid for all audiences who learn from a given identity-statement, of the difference it makes to the knowledge-state of each one of them. It is a *general* picture because in each case—in the map of *every* audience thus informed—the appropriate two...dots are replaced by one, and the total number of lines reduced by the elimination of duplicates. What we cannot do, of course, is give a detailed specification, valid for all audiences, of what lines are transferred and what eliminated as duplicates. This is what varies from audience to audience.

Coming to know the truth of a predicative statement involves adding something to the map. Further, anyone who is informed by a predication has, roughly, just the same addition made to his map as anyone else so informed. This does not hold true in the case of identity statements. Coming to know the truth of an identity statement involves eliminating something from the map. The bringing together of whatever information had attached to either of the two dots as attaching to only one is what I am referring to as the 'collative' function of identity statements. The informativeness of an identity statement consists not in any determinate cognitive content available to and invariant over all audiences who could be informed by it, but rather in a cognitive role or function it has of collating bodies of information, the content of which may vary quite a bit, but within limits, audience to audience. It is this that Strawson's knowledge-map model is meant to convey.

A second model, or picture, is offered by Strawson to display this functional difference between identities and predications. He says:[14]

> Imagine a man as, in part, a machine for receiving and storing knowledge of all items of which he already has some identifying knowledge. The machine contains cards, one card for each cluster of identifying knowledge in his possession. On receipt of an ordinary predication invoking one such cluster, the appropriate card is withdrawn, the new information is entered on it and the card is returned to stock. On receipt of an ordinary relational predication invoking two such clusters, the two appropriate cards are withdrawn, cross-referring entries are made on both and both cards are returned to stock. On receipt of an identity-statement invoking two such clusters, the two appropriate cards are withdrawn and a new card is prepared...incorporating the sum of the information contained in the original cards; the single card is returned to stock and the original cards are thrown away.

And, as in the case of the knowledge-map model, the increase in knowledge brought about by an informative identity statement is represented not by a process of simple addition, but by one of actual elimination:[15]

Here is a simple general procedure for modifying the machine's contents, common to all machines, all audiences, which are informed by the identity-statement. But of course the total number of entries in the machine's stock is not increased; if this number is altered at all, it is diminished, by the elimination of what turn out to be duplicate entries. And of course there is no single general account to be given of the entries summed on to the new card; this will vary from machine to machine.

Very similar to this machine model is an image presented by Michael Lockwood in his article 'Identity and Reference'. Lockwood suggests that the referential use of linguistic expressions can best be understood if we picture a person's epistemic state as consisting in his possession of bodies of information, or what he calls 'mental files', involving any item concerning which he has any knowledge or belief. These mental files are like Strawson's map dots, with their adjoined radiating lines, and even more like his machine cards, with their inscribed information. A person's epistemic state is altered linguistically when he accepts as true some statement to which he is audience, the making of which has involved the use of a referential expression which invokes, or in some way indicates, a mental file of his, into which the information conveyed by the statement is to be put. We can picture adding a card to the file, or augmenting the entry on some card already in the file.

But again, the function of an identity statement will be pictured differently from that of a predication. An identity statement will be informative for a hearer if and only if he possesses two distinct files of information given access to by the two referring expressions with which the identity is stated. Lockwood says:[16]

> The purpose of an identity statement, which will be fulfilled if it is accepted as true, is precisely to get the hearer to merge these files or bodies of information into one.

In Lockwood's model, as in Strawson's, the information contained in each of the initially distinct files may vary considerably hearer to hearer, audience to audience. And so the precise epistemic state resulting from the acceptance of a particular identity statement as true may vary considerably. But that state is effected in the same way, audience to audience. Thus, the generality we have attained by the use of these models has to do not with any specific cognitive content or determinate information conveyed by an identity statement, but with its cognitive or epistemic *function*.

It seems that we come to understand the informativeness of identity statements as they actually are uttered in ordinary contexts only when we cease to ask exactly *what* they inform us of, and turn rather to the question of *how* they inform us. But a complete answer to *this* question will yield a general indication of the kind of information collated by such a statement. Neither Strawson, nor Lockwood, nor for that matter any other philosopher who has caught a glimpse of the functional approach has even begun to spell this out adequately. But there must be some general constraints on what information is involved, on the components of the informational states which properly result from accepting any particular identity statement. Not just any collation of information can count as the acceptance, or back up the expression, of a particular identity claim. In order to see how identity statements function, we must come to see how their utterance involves bodies of information. To see this let us consider the case of an identity stated by means of two definite descriptions, and then one asserted by the use of two names.

Consider first one of the descriptions, used attributively, as actually satisfied by some object. The speaker and hearer both take a specific propertied individual to be picked out by its use. The question is, what information is invoked by the use of such a phrase in the context of an identity statement? This will constitute one of the two bodies of information to be collated or merged by the identity satement. We are asking whether any general characterisation can be given of the contents of that body of information.

For any audience so described, the information will be of three kinds. First, there will be whatever information is contained in the definite description itself. Secondly, there will be any information associated by the hearer with the description. These associations will be both logical and psychological, the former being more fundamental and less audience-relative. The logical associations will be between any term in the descriptive phrase and any sortals and determinables on which an understanding of its use depends. The psychological associations will involve any properties the hearer may believe must characterise, or most likely characterises, any object which satisfies such a description. And thirdly, the information invoked by a definite description so used will include any properties the hearer associates with, or believes to hold of, the particular object he believes to be in fact the unique denotatum of the description *as used*.

If the description is used in a non-standard, referential manner, it need not invoke the information which it standardly would be used to convey, as Donnellan has shown.[17] I can be informed by an utterance of the sentence 'The man sipping champagne is the host of this party' even if I know the person thus indicated to be drinking sparkling water. I need not accept the information standardly conveyed by the description as so used. The bodies of information collated or merged by my acceptance of the identity thus stated will not include any information that the man indicated is now sipping champagne. If the phrase were used attributively, my resultant epistemic state would involve not only this information, but such beliefs as that the host does not always abstain from alcohol, probably knows what champagne tastes like and so forth. And these related beliefs would depend on my acceptance of the description as so used. But the purely referential employment of a description need not work in this way.

So what information *is* invoked by such a referential act? First, any information necessary for the success of the reference. And secondly, any information associated by the hearer with the object to which in fact his attention has been drawn. And this is all.

This is a complete, and general, characterisation of the kinds of information invoked and collated by the utterance of an informative identity statement made by the use of definite descriptions. We thus have a better idea of what sorts of beliefs will be merged together by the acceptance of such an utterance as making a true statement. But now the case of identities stated with two proper names must be considered.

The question is how descriptive information concerning objects is invoked and collated by identity statements made with two names, as by a sentence such as S. We thus find ourselves confronting one of the most controversial areas in the philosophy of language—the theory of names, or more exactly, the question of how names are related to descriptive information. Fortunately, no full-blown theory will be necessary in order to answer our specific question. A minimal set of specifications will suffice.

It is necessary for my functional account of identity that I display some sort of connection between proper names and descriptive information such that a use of the former invokes or gives access to the latter. It is *not* necessary for me to claim that a name carries in itself descriptive information as an attributively used definite description does. In particular, I shall not claim that a name is a disguised or abbreviated description (Russell), or that it has a determinate descriptive sense (Frege), or that it is in any way equivalent to a cluster, or any sub-grouping of a cluster, of definite descriptions (a position often attributed to Searle). It is fortunate that my analysis of identity statements does not depend on any of these theories of names, as each of them is attended by very serious problems, the rehearsal of which will not be necessary here.[18]

I want to claim only that every name which has a use in ordinary language always is used, in its standard employment, under particular epistemic conditions and in association with some descriptive information, however, minimal the information, and however loose the association. There is at least one association which can in no sense be loose: The connection between a name and a sortal under which the name's bearer is individuated, and in association with which the name gets introduced into a language as a referring expression. Anyone who has command of the name 'Socrates', as used in philosophy, will know that Socrates is a person, a human being, and not a rock, a musical composition, or a color. If he lacks this information, then even though he may know that some English sentence such as 'Socrates was interesting' expresses a true statement, he will not know the truth expressed. He will not be able to make a full standard use of the name. Likewise, someone who has no idea what the names 'Hesperus' and 'Phosphorus' are used to refer to may be told, and may thus believe and even know, that the sentence 'Hesperus is Phosphorus' is used to make a statement which is true, but he will not thereby know the truth expressed. He cannot be said to know on that basis that Hesperus is Phosphorus. No one can be audience to S *as an informative identity statement* unless he is familiar with the appropriate sortal for each name, as such. This information, minimal as it is, necessarily is associated with any standard occurrence of a name in the context of an identity statement.[19]

Someone who has command of the name 'Socrates' as referring to a man may have almost any amount of correct or incorrect information associated with the bearer of that name, so long as the information is compatible with the sortal under which the name is used. He does have to be in the possession of *some* correct information, or we would not ascribe command of the name to him. But the information he must have, or may have, associated with the name is not specifiable in detail. For a person to be informed by an identity statement made with names, it is necessary that each name invoke for him some information, or body of information, and that the two names invoke two distinct bodies of information. However, the specific information invoked may vary considerably audience to audience. Ayer says:[20]

> Just as the names 'Dickens' and 'Boz' have no determinate sense, so the sentence 'Dickens is Boz' has no standard meaning. What proposition it is understood to express on any given occasion will depend on the answers which its interpreter has for the questions Who is Dickens? and Who is Boz? The information he receives will then be that one and the same person satisfies the whole range of predicates which these answers embody.

The identity statement will effect a collation or merging of bodies of information as information about one object, if it is accepted as true.

But, again, Ayer's way of putting the matter may be slightly misleading. No identity statement made with the use of proper names serves to predicate of some object, identifyingly referred to as a subject of predication, a pair of determinate, or completely specified and closed, sets of properties for *any* audience of the statement. Searle is thus mistaken when he says:[21]

'Everest is Chomolunga' states that the descriptive backing of both names is true of the same object.

There is no determinate instantiation of the definite description 'the descriptive backing of *a*', where '*a*' stands for any ordinary proper name in a natural language. And, as I have emphasised, the identity statement is not a predication. It has a different role and force.

The importance of identity

Any identity statement serves to license or warrant the merging or collating of all information associated with each of its referring expressions. This holds with regard not only to information previously associated with them, but also to future acquisitions of information. When I accept the truth of S, when I come to believe that Hesperus is Phosphorus, I accept everything I formerly have believed about Hesperus (excepting, of course, any belief implying that it is distinct from Phosphorus) as true of Phosphorus, and vice versa. I also subsequently shall associate any information received in connection with either one of any two referential expressions, or noun phrases, which *I* would use to state the identity, or in a context in which one of them has or would have its customary use, with the other expression as well, since I then would understand my use of them as co-referential.

The convoluted nature of the foregoing sentence was necessary in order to distinguish my position as carefully as possible from any version of the metalinguistic analysis of identity statements. I hold open the possibility of someone's coming to know, or knowing, an identity, without necessarily knowing any language, or having command of any referring linguistic expressions. All that would be required is that two distinct object individuations, or sets of individuations, have been made, and yet be believed to be appearances of only one entity. In such a case, neither any particular noun phrases, nor any linguistic expressions at all would be involved in the knowledge of the identity.

This point is crucial in recognising the importance of identity. Many philosophers, accepting either the objectual or the metalinguistic analysis of identity statements, have thought that the notion of identity is dispensable, at least in principle. For example, Quine has at one point suggested that identity statements are only the product of a peculiarity of language, and as such are in principle eliminable from language. In *Methods of Logic*, he says:[22]

... it is only because of a peculiarity of language that the notion of identity is needed. If our language were so perfect a copy of its subject matter that each thing had but one name, then statements of identity would indeed be useless.

But he also admits that 'such a language would be radically different from what we have', conceding that 'to rid language of redundant nomenclature' of certain types would be 'to strike at the roots' of language. He concludes:[23]

The utility of language lies partly in its failure to copy reality in any one-thing-one-name fashion. The notion of identity is then needed to take up the slack.

The attitude which seems to show through these remarks is that identity statements have a necessary role in language only in so far as we indulge in a very useful but theoretically unnecessary linguistic convention, the permissive allotment of multiple names to individual objects.

In the *Tractatus*, Wittgenstein shared this assessment of the role of identity statements, but in the severity of his search for an ideal notation, he considered, if not advocated, the rejection of the convention under which alone they have a use. He said:[24]

The identity sign, therefore, is not an essential constituent of conceptual notation.

Is identity thus eliminable, as Quine and Wittgenstein, in his early work, appear to have suggested? I think we can see quite easily that it is not. The conditions under which identity statements are useful, and even necessary, are not provided by a theoretically dispensable convention of language, but are inevitably a result of our epistemic situation in the world.

It would be an illusion generated by concentrating on artificial languages to think that we could have a functional natural language in which only one name is assigned to any named object. The conditions under which objects are individuated and referred to are so diverse, and the appearances of any object can be so varied, that any object which is named can be dubbed more than once without its being known that such a multiplicity of tagging has taken place. This is a necessary result of our epistemic condition. We are never presented with objects *in toto*, with all their many facets and appearances together. We have limited and incomplete access to anything we name. We may thus name an object twice, thinking we have named two different ones. Likewise, different people may call one and the same object by different names. The discovery that any such double tagging has taken place normally is expressed by the utterance of an identity statement.

This kind of situation is unavoidable. We do not have a constant number of nameable objects in the world and cannot have an exhaustive catalogue of names paired one-to-one with the objects, by means of which to talk about the world. Only under the conditions of the construction of an artificial language is such assignment of names to a limited domain of objects possible. Ordinary naming and the use of names is obviously not like that.

Furthermore, only a minute fraction of our references to items in the world is made by the use of names. Even if every named object had only one name, and we knew that to be the case, identity statements made with descriptive expressions would still be necessary. For every item in the world has more than one property. Thus, it may always be informative to say that some item which is identified by its having one property is the same as the object referred to by some other description. Objects can be, and are, singled out for our attention in a variety of ways. It is this set of conditions which provides for the usefulness and informativeness of identity statements.

However, just as I have held open the possibility that one might come to know identities without having a language at all, it may be contended that the importance, and even necessity, of the notion of identity for human thought can be shown independently of any considerations about language. Panayot Butchvarov has written:[26]

> But the apparent distinctness of material identicals is a fact about the world, or at least about our experience of the world, quite independent of language. This fact can be noticed and examined without reference to language. We need not name or describe . . . a planet we see at one time and a planet we see at another time, in order to wonder whether they are one and the same and perhaps determine that they are. The apparent distinctness . . . of the planets is a matter of experience, absolutely essential to the sort of situation we are confronted with, and not at all due to any names or descriptive phrases we apply to them. If it is to be understood, it must be understood as a fact about the world, not about language.

A quite similar insight can be gleaned from an article by H. N. Castañeda, entitled 'Identity and Sameness'.[27] There, Castañeda stresses that a proper understanding of statements made with sentences of the form 'a is the same as b' will depend on our recognition of the nature of our epistemic situation.[28] He draws a distinction between objects and what he calls 'guises of objects'.[29] According to his distinction, an object is an infinitely propertied individual which can never be presented to a finite observer *in toto*. We have access only to guises or presentations of these individuals. It thus is important to be able to recognize two guises as belonging to one object. It is such a recognition which is knowledge of an identity. This knowledge can be expressed by the utterance of a sentence of the form of S or (4), in which the two noun phrases are two names, each associated with one of the guises, or two descriptions, one of each guise. But it is possible for the knowledge to stand on its own, so to speak, apart from any such linguistic expression.

At this point it should be evident that synchronic identity statements have an ontological, as well as an epistemic, function. As I have shown, the epistemic function is that of collating or merging bodies of information. The related ontological function is one of reduction or simplification. Whereas, before coming to know a particular identity, we may have taken two bodies of information in our possession to be information about two different objects in the world, the cognitive change involved in recognising an identity results in our realising that they are bodies of information about only one object. In another place, Butchvarov says:[30]

> The general function of the concept of identity is to transform our experience into a world by reducing the objects of perception and thought to a smaller number of *entities*. . . . It is the most basic conceptual activity. . . . It consists in the enforcement of a sort of ontological parsimony, in a rendering of the objects of our perception and thought intelligible by means of simplifications.

The notion of identity, and the making of identity statements, thus constitutes a crucial part of the conceptual apparatus of any finite intelligence dealing with a world.

The views of Quine and Wittgenstein presented above seem to fail to take into account the inescapable nature of our epistemic situation. They appear to assume the possibility of a sort of Olympian access to the objects in the world which would allow us to recognise an object in any of its appearances and thus refer to it linguistically by means of only a single sign. This is not a possibility. And the role of identity statements in a language is much more important than their quoted remarks indicate. The functional analysis of identity makes this clear.

According to a functional analysis, an identity statement licenses or warrants the collating of bodies of information, both previously acquired and yet to be obtained. It does not predicate any particular property of any object or objects. Specifically, it does not attribute a logically simple, essential metaphysical property of synchronic self-identity to any object, nor does it assert any relation to hold between any two linguistic items.

5

Identity, Necessity, and Information

Information and analysis

In his posthumously published book, *The Varieties of Reference*, Gareth Evans has stated clearly his conviction that:[1]

> Once one's interest is in the phenomenon of language itself, one must be concerned with the way in which it functions as a means of communication among members of a community.

and that:[2]

> The central fact from which semanticists start is that a certain body of discourse is significant: it is effectively used for the expression and transmission of thoughts.

In my attempt to gain some clarity concerning identity statements, in my assessments of the objectual and metalinguistic analyses, as well as in my development of an alternative view, this has been my own concern and starting point. In seeking to attain a plausible philosophical account of identity statements, I have focused on the conceptual role, or informative value, of such statements as they standardly occur in natural languages. I thus have employed a procedure of philosophical analysis based on the assumption that, as Bede Rundle succinctly puts it, 'what is essentially determinative of present meaning is present usage'.[3]

The form of assertion known as an identity statement has a standard linguistic use. The utterance of such a statement normally is intended to perform a distinctive sort of informative function. The acceptance of an identity claim involves the effecting of that function among one's own informational states. The discovery of an identity, whether mediated linguistically or not, consists in a certain sort of merging or collating of different bodies of information. Identity statements cannot be understood unless this is understood. It is the informational or epistemic function of these statements which is the key to their proper analysis. When we have explicated this, we have given an account of their meaning.

I have argued that the objectual and metalinguistic analyses distort the informational value of identity statements. Their ordinary import is not accurately captured by either standard account. I have taken up and detailed a very different functional analysis precisely to accommodate that most salient feature of this important type of statement. My own account is built upon the conceptual role identity statements normally have. It thus clearly accords better with the facts of ordinary usage than the objectual and metalinguistic approaches. This is what commends it.

It could be argued that I have made too much of informational value in assessing the competing analyses. For example, I criticise the objectual account for assigning the same meaning or propositional content to S ('Hesperus is Phosphorus') and (1) ('Phosphorus is Phosphorus') by pointing out that S and (1) (understood as a duplicate identity) differ in informative import. But in his book *Ways of Meaning*, Mark Platts offers a common sort of argument that difference in informational content does not entail difference in meaning or propositional content.[4] Consider

 (i) Il pleut.

and

 (ii) It is raining.

For a monolingual English speaker, (i) and (ii) surely differ in informational content. Yet, just as surely, they express the same proposition, or are equivalent in meaning.

But of course in this case the difference in informational value is due only to linguistic incompetence. The difference in value between S and (1) has nothing to do with this sort of ignorance. One can understand both fully and yet be informed by only one of them. Their informational difference is of a sort which does entail that they differ in meaning in a semantically significant way. So the argument given by Platts leaves my procedure untouched.

There is another, larger scale and philosophically deeper, set of worries which some may have about the precise way in which I tie the analysis of identity statements to a particular range of facts concerning their standard transmission of information. What exactly is the semantic status of the resulting account? Are there broader philosophical and linguistic issues at stake in the acceptance of a functional analysis as providing in some central and important sense the meaning of identity statements? Am I, for example, taking up what seems to be among contemporary cognoscenti a minority stance with Gilbert Harmann that 'meaning depends on conceptual scheme rather than on truth conditions'?[5] Is the analysis of identity statements one battle in an ongoing war between, on the one side, truth-conditional or truth-theoretic semantics, and on the other side, non-truth-conditional or conceptual-role, or even speech-act semantics?

The objectual and metalinguistic analyses are obviously straight-forward applications of a truth-conditional semantics. On the meta-linguistic approach, the truth conditions are conditions of co-referentiality between linguistic expressions. On the objectual account, they are conditions of self-identity. These are the only purely truth-conditional accounts available. So their implausibilities are implausibilities for an exclusive use of that sort of semantic analysis.

In highly controversial matters disputed by intelligent and well informed parties, it is sometimes wise to be as ecumenical as possible. In this spirit we might be inclined to make the following assignments. The metalinguistic analysis successfully gives us the conditions under which, and under which alone, the assertive utterance of a sentence of the appropriate form is the making of an identity statement. The objectual analysis gives us the conditions under which any such statement is true. And the functional analysis provides a pragmatics, or performative account, of what transpires in the successful expression or acceptance of such a claim. Only an understanding of all three analyses will give us a complete understanding of identity statements.

Such ecumenism is tempting. We seem to have a neat and quite complementary division of analytic labour in this taxonomy. But focus for a moment on the role therein allotted to the objectual analysis. It is supposed to provide the truth conditions for identity statements. In order to help us see whether it succeeds in doing this, let us ask a few simple questions.

If Mary Ann Evans never had chosen to write, would it still be true that George Eliot was Mary Ann Evans? If Venus had had a very different orbit around the sun, such that it was not the first celestial object visible in the evenings from earth, or the last nocturnal light to disappear in the mornings, or better yet, if the earth and its dwellers had never existed, would Hesperus still have been Phosphorus? Finally, if someone knew Samuel Clemens personally without ever having read any of his writings and without ever coming across the name 'Mark Twain', would he thereby know that Mark Twain was one and the same person as Samuel Clemens? Or would he know *of* Clemens that he was Twain? To each of these questions, the objectual analysis as an account of truth conditions yields a clear affirmative answer.

But to any one who is not fully imbued with all the usual concomitants of a direct theory of reference, to anyone who does not have his intuitions already informed by the dictates of an objectual analysis, this can all seem quite dubious. In his book *Grammar in Philosophy*, Rundle begins by pointing out that:[6]

> General accounts of the workings of language reveal philosophers under considerable pressure to find matching items for words, phrases, and even whole sentences: proper names are mapped onto persons or things named, adjectival and verbal phrases onto properties and states, and declarative sentences, when true, onto their corresponding facts.

What is *the fact* stated by a true identity statement? Is it, as the objectual analysis stipulates, the fact that an object is identical with itself? Why think there is a single such fact stated at all? If this does not enter into what is standardly *communicated* or expressed by an identity statement, why follow the objectual analysis into holding that there is such a determinate fact that constitutes the truth condition for the statement? Why not resist the general pressure to find a simple 'matching item' here? Once we have a functional account of identity statements, once we are clear on their conceptual role, I can see no reason at all to be seduced by a general semantic strategy into thinking that there must be a single fact of identity rendering any such statement true.

This is not to say that there are nothing like truth conditions for identity statements. In the next chapter, I want to propose that Leibniz's Law is best understood as giving us something like the truth conditions, or more precisely, the conditions of warranted assertability, for identity statements. It is better understood as having this role than as serving to define or govern a relation of identity. I do not intend here to impugn in any wholesale way the usefulness or importance of truth-conditional semantics in some contexts. Nor do I want to suggest that a concern for something like truth conditions is wholly irrelevant to an understanding of identity statements. What I do deny is that the objectual analysis gives us a specification of those conditions. Although it is a widely accepted account, it fails to offer a plausible delineation of any single fact expressed by identity statements.

So the functional account of the last chapter is not to be thought of as just one of three different and equally respectable analyses, each of which plays a distinctive role in our understanding of identity statements. The metalinguistic analysis does give us conditions under which a sentence can be uttered to express a true identity statement. But it does not throw much light on identity statements themselves unless it is developed in such a way as to lead us on to abandon it and embrace instead the functional account, which preserves its insights without retaining its weaknesses. Thus, I present the functional analysis as alone sufficient for a full understanding of identity statements as they occur in natural languages. It has been anticipated and adumbrated by a few philosophers, whose relatively brief remarks I have quoted nearly in full in the text and notes of the last chapter. But it has not been clearly seen as a full-blown alternative analysis of identity statements. As indicated in chapter three, it is attained as a self-sufficient account of identity statements only after a basic assumption about these statements is rejected and a common method of their analysis eschewed. And none of the philosophers who over the last decade have glimpsed the basic elements of the functional approach has recognized or made clear the full implications of these changes. Particularly interesting is the new perspective they give us for our understanding of the notion or concept of identity.

Synchronic self-identity

Many contemporary philosophers are convinced that it is an object's exemplification of identity, its being-identical-with-itself, or its synchronic self-identity, which renders any synchronic identity statement about it true. In chapters one and three I have suggested that we have no good reason at all to believe that there is any such property as the logically simple one termed reflexive relation 'identity' is generally supposed to denote. It has been most common for philosophers to start with an understanding of such a property or relation of identity and then analyse identity statements as asserting this to hold in particular cases. I have suggested that we can get clear about identity and identity statements only if we abandon this procedure and attend directly to the standard role of these statements in the expression and communication of thoughts. There is no distinct concept of identity which is a component of, or is imbedded in, standard identity statements. Such a notion can be constructed with the principles of reflexivity, symmetry, transitivity, and Leibniz's Law, but it has nothing to do with our common understanding of identity statements.

If the switch to a functional analysis of identity statements involved the flat denial that there is any property at all denoted by the terms 'identity' or 'self-identity', this could be seen by some as an even less plausible commitment than any entailed by the objectual and metalinguistic analyses. Whereas they seemed to distort ordinary usage, this claim seems to run counter to the most minimal and respectable sort of metaphysics. But in fact it should be clear that the functional analysis itself has no such metaphysical involvements at all. It does not rule out there being such a property as identity or self-identity. The relation between the functional account and such metaphysical matters is much looser. If we have serious doubts about there being the sort of property or relation philosophers traditionally have taken identity to be, we thereby have some motivation to consider an analysis of identity statements which does not require such a property. And if we accept a functional analysis, we lose a major motivation, if not the sole traditional one, for acknowledging the existence of such a property or relation.

So my account of identity statements does not require that I repudiate any sort of identity property at all. However, as has become clear, I have serious doubts about a certain sort of alleged property of identity. And I have spelled out those doubts to some extent, since any proper grounding they have is a ground for relinquishing the understanding of identity statements most common nowadays among philosophers, the objectual analysis.

In fact, all I want to deny metaphysically is that there is a distinct, logically simple property of identity, or self-identity, or identity-with-*a*, where *a* is any object. But when this is denied, nothing is lost except a metaphysical illusion and the central ingredient in a popular, distorting perspective on identity statements. Identity through time, for instance, is not the having of a logically simple property of identity over a series of moments. An object's identity through time is just its continuity in existence. And the much discussed 'trans-world identity' is not an object's retention of a logically simple property of identity from one possible world to another. Trans-world identity is just stipulative counterfactual existence. Or, better, it is just the consistency of an object's essential properties with a variety of possible accidents, understood in a certain way. No 'core' property of identity is needed to give us either diachronic or trans-world identity, the two most important identity notions in contemporary metaphysics. So nothing of metaphysical importance in these areas is lost if it is denied that there is any such property at all.

After constructing an argument which makes liberal use of identity properties, Alvin Plantinga once wrote:[7]

> Indeed, is there any reason to suppose that 'being identical with Socrates' names a property? Well, is there any reason to suppose it does not? I cannot think of any, nor have I heard any that are at all impressive. To be sure, one hears expressions of a sort of nebulous discomfort; when asked to believe that there is such a property as *being identical with Socrates*, philosophers often adopt an air of wise and cautious skepticism. But this does not constitute an objection.

There are of course philosophers who have argued that there is *no* sense of 'self-identity' which expresses a property of any sort, nor any sense of the predicate form ⌜identical-with-*a*⌝ which expresses an attribute of any kind. D M Armstrong, for example, argues that there is no need for recognising such a property in any scientific account of the world, and thus no place for it in our ontology.[8] I incline to agree with Plantinga that reasons such as this are not all that impressive. For why should strictly scientific theorizing supply the only source for our ontological commitments?

On the other hand, Armstrong's position is just an application of Ockhamist scruples about superfluous postulations in our ontology. Although I dissent from a number of the particulars of his application of this perspective, it is in general a very reasonable one. And in so far as it can be argued persuasively that Ockhamist caution is an important element in any successful attempt to know and understand the world,[9] any sort of 'self-identity' which is ruled out from this point of view has against it at least one sort of reason which is fairly impressive.

I have contended that there is no distinct, logically simple property of identity or self-identity which is predicated of objects in identity statements. I have intended this denial as two-fold: (i) Identity statements do not state that a discrete, logically simple property of identity is instantiated, and (ii) There is no such property at all. Neither of these claims is entailed by the functional analysis of identity statements. So my account does not stand or fall with their truth. They can, however, serve as components of an overall view of identity and identity statements in which the functional account would play an important role. If these denials appear plausible, they can incline one toward a functional account of identity statements. Conversely, any appeal that the function account has can incline one toward accepting these claims.

Now that my denials are properly registered, I should say something in a more positive vein about the metaphysics of identity. I do want to allow that there is a legitimate synchronic sense of the terms 'identity' and 'self-identity', a sense which does not purport to denote a logically simple property. On this understanding, an object's self-identity, or its identity, is just its overall *essence*, a maximal set of logically simple properties individually necessary and jointly sufficient for *its* existence (where the necessity involved is of the broadly logical sort). On this view, the (degenerate) proposition that everything is self-identical would amount to no more than something like the triviality that everything has whatever essential properties it has. And Socrateity, or the property of being identical with Socrates, would be just the haecceity, or individual essence, of Socrates, a property most perspicuously expressed not by a two-place predicate, which gives the illusion of denoting a relational property (identity), but by a one-place, non-relational predicate.

Although this sort of identity, or self-identity, is ontologically admissible on some theoretical grounds supporting essentialism, we still have no reason to think that identity statements, as standardly used in natural languages, have anything to do with it at all. The acceptance of the essentialist postulation certainly gives us no such reason. As L Jonathan Cohen reminds us in another context, 'Metaphysics should not be allowed to intrude into the semantics of natural languages.'[10] Identities, or self-identities, in the sense of maximal individual essences, are not properties predicated of objects in ordinary identity statements. And there is no plausible argument which gets us from the occurrence of those statements in natural languages to the existence of such properties. Their postulation is independently motivated. They are objects of metaphysical reflection whose existence is not evinced in ordinary language by identity statements.

In contrast with logically composite haecceities, there is no good reason at all for the postuation or countenancing of logically simple, metaphysically distinct property of self-identity or identity, as a great many philosophers have understood it. And this has a mildly troublesome consequence for some essentialists. When asked by doubters to give examples of essential properties, essentialists easily come up with fairly plausible lists of kind-essential properties. On current theory, it is essential, for instance, to being water that a stuff contain hydrogen. Animality is essential for being a tiger, and so forth. But when pressed to give examples of properties essential to individuals which are not general kind-essential properties, many essentialists rely on such items as Socrateity, or the property of being-identical-with-Socrates. And surely that is not what the doubter is looking for. Presumably, what is wanted is an example of some logically simple property which distinctively goes into making up part of an individual essence. A mere mention of 'Socrateity' will not do the job here. In order to satisfy their questioners, essentialists will have to provide examples of a different sort, a task which is not nearly so easy. This is due to 'Socrateity' denoting no logically simple property, but rather acting as a sort of abbreviation for the maximal set of properties fundamentally essential to Socrates, whatever they are.

There is thus a sense in which it can be allowed that there is a property of self-identity (a logically composite property), and an important sense, the one assumed by many philosophers, in which 'self-identity' fails to pick out a property (the sense in which it fails to denote a logically simple property). Armstrong, however, has offered two reasons for denying that there is any property of self-identity at all, in any sense. These considerations might be thought by some to block the sort of position I want to take, countenancing one sense of 'self-identity' and repudiating another. However, I think it can be seen quite easily that in so far as his reasoning can be taken to be to any extent plausible, it allows what I allow, while disallowing exactly what I disallow.

Armstrong begins his discussion by saying:[11]

First, we know *a priori* that a thing must be identical with itself. Now if we take seriously the idea that what properties there are is a matter for scientific investigation, then the existence of this *a priori* knowledge is a good reason for denying that *being identical with itself* is a property.

A number of highly controversial philosophical assumptions lie behind this argument as it stands. Most I shall pass over, but I believe that a qualification or restriction of his remarks in at least two respects would make the reasoning here palatable to many more people. First, there need be no reference to specifically *scientific* investigation (of course, then it would not be characteristically Armstrongian). And secondly, the principle here needs restriction to concrete (non-abstract) particulars. Then the rule specified would be that we view a predicate, whose significance range is concrete particulars, to express a property only if ascriptions of that predicate to particulars issue in propositions with *a posteriori* truth value (one could know the subject of the ascription without knowing *a priori* the truth of the predication). There is some intuitive backing for the claim that real properties of concrete objects are the sorts of things appropriate to investigation and *a posteriori* discovery. If on the basis of such intuitions the qualified principle were found plausible and employed, it would rule out a logically simple, discrete property of self-identity, but not self-identity as an object's particular set of logically simple, essential properties.

If ordinary identity statements predicated simple self-identity of objects, then some statements of such identity could be investigated and discovered *a posteriori* to be true. But the *a posteriori* discovery would not be, as Plantinga, Kripke, Stalnaker, and Tichy, among others, have realised, the discovery that that property held of an object. And of course, ordinary identity statements just do not serve to predicate such a property in the first place. So Armstrong's revised principle would rule out a logically simple property of identity, the sort of property I see absolutely no good reason to countenance.

But it would not rule out an object's having a particular maximal set of simple essential properties. For it seems that we could investigate Socrates' essential properties and discover *a posteriori* that he had certain ones rather than others. This is true in case haecceities include such properties as that of particular origin, for example. So Armstrong's revised principle arguably would allow into our ontology the sort of self-identity I am prepared to allow.

The same is true of the second reason Armstrong presents for repudiating any property of self-identity. He proposes what he characterises as a 'plausible necessary condition for something's being a property', saying:[12]

> If a particular has a property, that property must endow the particular with some specific causal power, or if the property is causally idle, then it must at least be an intelligible hypothesis that the property should endow particulars with some specific causal power.

He concludes by saying:

> Now could a thing's identity with itself even be conceived to endow the object with causal power? It is difficult to see how it could.

Again, if we are to have here a principle which could be of any significant plausibility to many people at all, we would have to restrict it and qualify it. For instance, we would have to limit it again to concrete particulars and their properties. But any version retaining the general spirit of Armstrong's formulation would rule out synchronic self-identity as a logically simple, distinct metaphysical property. It would not, however, rule out the sort of self-identity I am willing to admit. For many essentialists consider the haecceities of physical objects to involve such properties as fundamental genetic or molecular constitution, properties obviously relevant to causal powers. Likewise, the haecceities of persons would involve powers of mind relevant to causation of some type.

The point of bringing up Armstrong's remarks is not to discuss them in any detail, and is not to endorse them either. I mention them here only to show that a fairly well known pair of arguments for denying that 'self-identity' denotes a property is compatible with the position I am espousing, and does not undermine my allowance for a legitimate sense of 'self-identity'. Acknowledging a composite metaphysical property of self-identity is compatible with a number of grounds for denying a logically simple property of identity, and is compatible with a functional analysis of identity statements. The crucial point to keep in mind, however, is that identity statements are not statements that this sort of essentialist property is exemplified. Paradoxically, identity and identity statements must be kept apart if we are to be clear on either. They have little to do with each other.

A problem of modality

On any theory of essentialism which countenances haecceities, an object exemplifies its essence with at least what Kripke calls 'weak necessity'. It is in this sense necessarily true of anything that exists that it is self-identical. But once we admit a modal property of necessary self-identity, or of, say, necessary identity-with-a, there is a well known proof that all true identity statements are necessarily true, originally constructed by Ruth Barcan (now Ruth Barcan Marcus).[13] For suppose that Hesperus is Phosphorus. A property of Phosphorus will be necessary-identity-with-Phosphorus. On Leibniz's Law, every property of Phosphorus must be a property of Hesperus, including, presumably, this modal property. But to say that Hesperus has the property of being necessarily identical with Phosphorus is just to say that the statement that Hesperus is identical with Phosphorus has the modal value of weak necessity. It is thus in this sense necessarily true.

This argument could be thought to create a difficulty for the functional analysis of identity statements. For on that account, an identity statement just brings together two bodies of information as information about one object. That information typically will involve such descriptions as 'the first celestial object to appear in the evenings' and 'the last luminous body to leave the early morning sky'. But these are the sorts of descriptions which express properties only contingently exemplified by objects. Consequently, as I earlier have quoted Ayer as holding, it can be concluded that the 'cash value' of a typical identity statement has the modal status of contingency, not necessity. So we seem to have a problem. We have a deductive argument which seems to prove that all identity statements are necessary. And we have an analysis of such statements which seems to imply that a great many of them are contingent.

In addressing this problem, something should be said first about the modal status of the information collated by identity statements. In his interesting article, 'The Boethian Compromise', Plantinga has proposed the view that proper names express essences of objects by virtue of a semantic tie with world-indexed definite descriptions, descriptions of the form ⌜the F in W⌝ where ⌜W⌝ designates rigidly a possible world. These descriptions are intended by Plantinga to denote world-indexed properties, for example the property of appearing first in the evening sky in α, where 'α' designates the actual world. Now, the notion of a world-indexed property is somewhat controversial, but it seems to have the status Plantinga ascribes to 'being-identical-with-Socrates' in the passage quoted earlier—there are philosophers who find such a property dubious, but so far as I know, no one has constructed an argument which plausibly throws them into question.[14] The relevance of world-indexing is this: The bodies of information collated by the identity statement that Hesperus is Phosphorus or that Mark Twain is Samuel Clemens, can be understood *either* as involving many descriptions or properties holding only contingently of the planet or the man, or else can be understood as embodying the α-transforms of those descriptions or properties. The α-transform of a property is the property formed by indexing it rigidly to the actual world. And surely, when we believe that Twain was the author of *Huckleberry*

Finn, we believe that he was the author of *Huckleberry Finn in the actual world* ('in α'). If this is the way the information collated by identity statements is understood, we seem to lose any motivation for ascribing to them the modal status of contingency, and the functional account is clearly reconciled to the Barcan proof.

However, this view of information collated in identity statements need not be adopted at this point to solve our problem. It can be argued that there would be at least one fundamental flaw in any use of the well known proof to create a problem of consistency for the combination of views I am allowing. First of all, the proof produces a modal identity property from one form of identity statement, and then uses that property to construct another identity claim with the modal status of necessity. The property of self-identity which I recognize could be extracted from contexts of the form '$a = a$' only by assuming that '$a = a$' provides a purely referential context of common semantic form in which part of the sentence refers to an object, and the rest of the sentence signifies some property predicated of that object. But on the position I am espousing, abstraction of identity properties from identity statements is disallowed. Thus, from the truth that Mark Twain was Sam Clemens, we cannot abstract the property of being identical with Clemens. There is no such property conveyed by the statement.

It would not be sufficiently perspicuous and accurate to try to express this point by saying that '$a = a$' does not entail that a has the property of being identical with a, and that '$\square(a = a)$' does not entail that a has the property standardly represented as '$\square(a = \quad)$'. For if '$a = a$' expresses a true statement, then if we allow self-identity to be an essential property of every object in our ontology, it does follow that '$a = a$' entails that a has the property of self-identity, not because the identity sentence '$a = a$' is used to assert such a property of its object, but merely because it would be impossible for the statement to be true and yet a to lack self-identity. For the statement to be true, a must exist. And in order for that to be the case, a must exemplify whatever its set of basic essential properties is; that is to say, it must be self-identical.

So the entailment holds if '$a = a$' expresses a true statement. But if '$a = a$' is a duplicate identity, formed by reflexivity alone operating on a single semantic type, I have suggested we have no reason to see it as expressing a statement or proposition at all (this is indicated late in chapter one, and implied by the functional analysis). In that case, the argument would be blocked, for there would be no two propositions between which the entailment relation could hold. Further, for the proof we need '$\square(a = a)$' to express a true statement. If I am right, this would be so only if '$a = a$' were not a duplicate identity, that is, only if the two occurrence of 'a'

represented two different semantic types of the same word or phrase type. But then to assume that '$\Box(a = a)$' is true is just to beg the question against anyone not already convinced of the conclusion of the Barcan proof, which is intended to show that any identity statement, however informative it might seem and however contingent it might look, is necessary.

But I am convinced that the use of this proof to create a problem of consistency for my view is most obviously flawed in the following way. The proof employs a notion of self-identity expressed by the predicate form ⌜is identical with a⌝. I have granted that an object's identity or self-identity can be seen as its individual essence, or haecceity. Let us denote the modal property of being necessarily identical to Phosphorus by 'PH'. Phosphorus has PH. In light of the truth of S ('Hesperus is Phosphorus'), Hesperus has PH. In each of the last two sentences, it has been stated that a certain object exemplifies a certain haecceity. How is this relevant at all to the modal status of ordinary identity statements? If they asserted something about haecceity exemplification, if they served to predicate individual essences of objects, it would be relevant. But identity statements can be understood most plausibly to have no such assertive content at all.

The 'proof' of the necessity of identity statements trades on something like equivocation with the sign '=' as it usually is presented by writers like Kripke, and with less formal identity expressions in the version I sketched above. The necessary identity which is admissible in certain theories of essentialism just has no direct relevance to the content or modal status of ordinary identity statements. Thus, my allowance that there is such a logically complex property does not have results incompatible with any clear implication of the functional analysis of identity statements. That analysis can stand alongside a metaphysic of individual essences.

Part Two

ASSESSING IDENTITY STATEMENTS

6

Leibniz's Law

One commonly hears philosophers say that identity is a relation 'governed by' Leibniz's Law. Unfortunately, what they often mean is that one (or more) of what they themselves sometimes fail to distinguish as at least three distinct principles provides (or provide) the conditions under which an identity relation holds, or under which any identity statement is true. In some cases, the name 'Leibniz's Law' is used to refer loosely and collectively to them all. I shall sketch out the differences and similarities among these principles first, and then go on to suggest what the alleged relation of 'governing' amounts to in the case of identity statements. It will be argued that these principles relate to their epistemic status. They display the conditions under which we assert or deny identities.

The problematic principles

The principle of the indiscernibility of identicals, which I shall refer to as 'L1', presents a necessary condition for identity. It states that for any object x and any object y, x is identical with y only if every property had by x is had by y, and vice versa. Identicals must share all properties in common. The quite different principle of the identity of indiscernibles proposes that the complete commonality of properties is sufficient for identity. This principle, L2, states that for any object x and any object y, if every property of x is property of y and vice versa, then x is identical with y. And there is, of course, the conjunction of these two principles, which would display necessary and sufficient conditions for identity.

A further different principle is that of substitutivity. Whereas the former two principles, L1 and L2, mention objects and their properties, this principle, L3, stipulates a rule concerning the use of the linguistic expressions in identity statements. Richard Cartwright has presented the following rough formulation of the principle of substitutivity:[1]

For all expressions α and β, $\ulcorner \alpha = \beta \urcorner$ expresses a true proposition if and only if, for all sentences S and S', if S' is like S save for containing an occurrence of β where S contains an occurrence of α, then S expresses a true proposition only if S' does also.

Now these three principles have not all been equally acceptable to philosophers. To say that L3, substitutivity, has its detractors would be an understatement. Linsky and Cartwright, for example, have declared that it is just false, adducing apparent counter-examples to demonstrate this. And L2 has been surrounded by significant controversy over whether two objects could not differ in number only, sharing all their (non-trivial) properties in common. It is at least not utterly obvious that complete qualitative identity amounts to quantitative or numerical identity. But it has seemed obvious to many philosophers that strict numerical identity involves qualitative identity. Thus, L1, the indiscernibility of identicals, is the least controverted of the forms of Leibniz's Law. Wiggins, for example, has expressed the feeling that it is as obvious as the law of non-contradiction.[2] Cartwright has suggested that it is a self-evident truth.[3] A very brief look at some of these misgivings, criticisms, and positive assessments of the various forms of Leibniz's Law will give us some indication as to which are defensible, and as to how they function with regard to the making and evaluating of ordinary identity statements.

Let us look first at L1, the principle of the indiscernibility of identicals. It is interesting to note that the normal context in which this principle is propounded and discussed is one in which the objectual analysis of identity statements is taken for granted. From this perspective, David Wiggins attempts to display what he considers the obviousness of the principle by writing that he is tempted merely to ask:[4]

How if a is b could there be something true of *the object a* which was untrue of *the object b*? After all, *they are the same object.*

On an objectual analysis of identity, L1 would seem to state no more than that any object which is self-identical has whatever properties it has. But this, though obviously true, is totally vacuous. It tells us nothing. L1 has always been thought to say more than *this*; that is, to say *something*. The unreflective way many people might be tempted to specify this 'more' is by saying:

If two objects are identical, then they *must* share all their properties in common.

In fact, Benson Mates *has* said precisely this.[5] Wiggins' use of the grammatical plural to refer to what is, *ex hypothesi*, one object, as well as

Mates' talk of 'two objects' which are identical gives us the illusion that something of substance is being said with L1. But, of course, the Mates statement would be true and interesting only if qualitative identity, or complete similarity, were under discussion. Made with regard to numerical or strict identity, the antecedent of his statement is logically false, so the assertion as a whole is uninformative.

So what does L1 tell us about identity? That an object is self-identical only if it has all and only its own properties? If my suggestions in earlier chapters are correct, no identity statement predicates self-identity of an object. So if L1 specifies a necessary condition for the truth of any identity statement, it does not thereby offer a condition for the self-identity of any object. On a metalinguistic analysis of identity, L1 would be thought to stipulate a necessary condition for the co-referentiality of two referring expressions. But again this would be the uninteresting and lax condition that their alleged common referent have all and only its own properties. This analysis of identity statements I also have rejected. So the interesting question is: What does L1 amount to, given my preferred functional account of identity assertions? This can be seen clearly only after looking at L2 for a moment.

L2 amounts simply to the claim that two objects cannot share all their non-trivial properties in common. By 'non-trivial' I and most philosophers mean to exclude such dubious properties as 'identity with x' or 'difference from y'. As I have mentioned, this claim has been debated and denied.[6] And again, it is not completely clear what is being alleged in the principle to be a sufficient condition for identity. It is not to be understood as proposing a condition under which two objects are one object. Is it simply displaying the kind of condition under which we have to do with one single object? If so, then what is the condition? Some object's having all and only its own properties? We can see how hard it is to state L1 and L2 so that they appear to say anything at all which could be both true and interesting. But their basic thrust can be seen if we approach them from a different direction.

The warranting of identities

Let us look at what the normal, or even paradigmatic, conditions are under which we assert or accept identity statements as true. Recall the discussion of chapter four. It often may be the case that we are acquainted with an object in two different contexts, or two different sets of circumstances, and, seeing it in sufficiently different guises, are not aware that in fact it is a single object with which we are thus acquainted. We have two distinct 'mental files' on that one subject, mistakenly assuming them to relate to two different objects. It is such an epistemic set-up that allows for the informative utterance of an identity statement. In such a context, we may come to know an identity. This comes about when the two mental files coincide in enough information, or in any amount of the right kind of information for the sort of object in question, that we see them as both pertaining to one and the same thing. We realise that it is with only one object, not two, that we have to do.

L2 can be taken as an attempt to display the ideal contents of our cognitive state which would be sufficient in any case to warrant as strongly as possible the assertion or acceptance of an identity statement. Taken in this way, it is a principle for the warranted assertability of identity statements. It is viewed in its normal epistemic role rather than in some metaphysical, uniquely philosophical role. And it is only with regard to the latter kind of function that it has elicited controversy in the literature.

I think it is obvious that all normal statements of identity proceed from a cognitive awareness of qualitative identity. We have no access to objects apart from our access to their properties. And when there is sufficient coincidence of property information between two mental files, we *do* consider ourselves warranted in asserting an identity statement, using a referring expression imbedded in, or associated with, each of those files to make the statement. Taken in this sense, I think the sort of principle indicated by L2 should be uncontroversial. Now, a meticulous formulation of it as an epistemic principle would differ significantly from, and be more complex than, its traditional presentations. For example, reference would not be made to 'all properties', or even to 'all non-trivial properties'. As David Shwayder has written:[7]

> ... little if any sense can be attached to such expressions as 'A and B are alike in respect to all properties', if this is the unlimited philosophical 'all' ... for no one, even in principle, can list off these properties for any particular object.

I have suggested that it is when two mental files coincide in 'enough' information, or in any amount of information 'of the right kind', that we judge them to pertain to one and the same object. And no more exact specification can be given in general. What counts as enough information or as information of the right kind will vary in accordance with the kind of object in question. Shwayder, again, has said that:[8]

> ... we cannot say in advance what particular sorts of properties and relations will be relevant for establishing identity and difference in each and every case.

We might say that the coincidence of mental file contents sufficient for identity is at least to some significant extent sortal relative, or relative to the unification criteria for the kind of object in question.

Principle L1 can be taken to spell out the collating function of identity statements. The acknowledgement of an identity involves the merging together of two bodies of information as information about one object. Allowing ourselves to speak loosely of the referent of a mental file as that object the information of that file is information about, we can say that the merging together of two files is possible only if the referent of either of them has all the properties ensconced as the information content of the other (excluding of course any conveyed by false beliefs which entail that the files do not share a single referent, or any held previously to characterise the referent of the file only on the basis of such a false assumption). Unless there is an object with all, or enough, of the properties of both files, no identity statement made with two referring expressions drawn from the two files, one from each, will be acceptable.

Again, this can be seen as an epistemic principle for the warranted assertability of identity statements. Given sufficient qualifications, it can be said that difference in properties implies difference of property bearer. And, of course, this is just the transposition of L1. L1 can also be taken to convey the performative force of an identity statement. The acceptance of such a statement involves the collating of properties from each of two bodies of information as properties of one object. In this respect, L1 goes further than L2. L2 says that with sufficient coincidence of *present* information, the collating of mental files, the recognition of an identity, is warranted. L1 not only presents such a present coincidence as necessary, but indicates that any *new* information which would have gone into one or the other of the two previously distinct files must be such as to fit well with the other in the now single file, the result of the merger of identity. If this is not possible, the alleged identity must be disavowed, the identity statement rejected.

Substitutivity

Thus, these two principles of Leibniz's Law can be seen to function so as to determine the epistemic status of identity statements. As long as L2 is satisfied, and L1 is not violated, an identity statement is warranted, or grounded. And, likewise, L3 can be seen to play this same role. As I have mentioned, some philosophers who accept one or both of L1 and L2 want to say that L3 is unacceptable. But, as Ruth Marcus has pointed out, the roles of L3, and the conjunction of L1 and L2, in first and second order predicate logic, respectively, clearly show that they come to the same thing.[9]

It may even be suggested that the principle of substitutivity more perspicuously displays that role. Whereas L1 and L2 purport to talk of objects and properties, L3 concerns the linguistic representations of objects and properties. And, consonant with our model of mental files, linguistic representations can be said to constitute the contents, or at least the available form of the contents, of a mental file.[10] We judge identities from the perspective of our *beliefs* about objects and their properties. And granting that beliefs are expressible in the making of statements with sentences of natural languages, L3 contains a more explicit recognition of this than do L1 and L2. Of course, it might be said that we need a principle to specify the conditions under which there *is* an identity, not just under which we are warranted in asserting one. This L1 and L2 are thought to do. What does an identity consist in? An object's having all and only its own properties? No, in relation to identity statements it consists in an object's having any set of appearances and properties such that they might be thought (mistakenly but reasonably) to characterise two different objects. It consists in the possibility of two mental files being held on one object. If we can break the illusion that synchronic, numerical identity is a logically simple property characterising objects independent of any relation between objects and their perceivers, we can see this. No principles are needed to tell us when objects are identical. We need to know only when the assertion of an identity statement is warranted, or unwarranted.

The warranting conditions, or even the truth conditions, of an identity statement will not be merely conditions having to do with objects and their properties. The conditions will also involve what I am referring to, loosely, as 'linguistic representations'. And L3 captures this.

L3, the principle of substitutivity, thus can be seen also as an epistemic principle for the grounding of identity statements. But, of course, as I have mentioned earlier, this form of Leibniz's Law has its detractors. The alleged counter-examples they produce fall roughly into three categories. First, there are the contexts of substitution involving modal operators, such as 'necessarily'. A well known case is provided by the following three sentences:[11]

(1)   9 is the number of the planets.
(2)   9 is necessarily greater than 7.
(3)   The number of the planets is necessarily greater than 7.

(2) is true. If (1) is a true identity, then, according to L3, (3) should be true as well. But it is not. The number of the planets could have been less than 7, if, for example, there had been only five planets. So we have a case in which the substitution of one expression for an apparently co-referential one leads us from a truth to a falsehood, in violation of L3.

Secondly, there are intensional contexts of substitution. An example would be:[12]

(4)   Cicero is Tully.
(5)   Philip believes that Cicero denounced Catiline.
(6)   Philip believes that Tully denounced Catiline.

It seems entirely possible that (4) and (5) be true, and yet that Philip without inconsistency denies or doubts the claim that Tully denounced Catiline. He would do this, of course, only if he did not know the truth of (4). But what is important in assessing the principle L3 is that it is possible for (4) to be true, and yet that the inter-substitution of the two co-referential expressions in (4) not lead from truths to truths in all statement making contexts. This is contrary to L3.

Thirdly, there is a less well defined category of apparent counter-examples involving contexts whose logical form is not readily evident. A notorious example is:[13]

(7)   Giorgione is Barbarelli.
(8)   Giorgione is so-called because of his size.
(9)   Barbarelli is so-called because of his size.

Here again we have a substitution of co-referential expressions leading from a truth to a falsehood.

It has been contended by Marcus that the principle of substitutivity applies to, and thus should be tested by its ability to handle, only contexts in which statements are presented in clear logical form.[14] For example, when the predicate 'is so-called because of his size' is put into logical form, it becomes 'is called "Giorgione" because of his size'. And *this* predicate yields a true statement when attached to either 'Giorgione' or 'Barbarelli'. In light of the possibility that the apparent failure of substitutivity between co-referential expressions in modal and intensional contexts is to be explained in the same way, as due to ambiguities in logical form, Marcus has re-stated the principle in the following way:[15]

> For all proper names α and β (indexed to preserve univocality), $\ulcorner \alpha = \beta \urcorner$ expresses a true proposition just in case for all sentences P, S, and S', if S is a restatement of P in logical form, and if S' is like S save for containing an occurrence of β where S contains an occurrence of α, then S expresses a true proposition only if S' does also.

As explained in the last chapter, I do not restrict the referring expressions in identity statements to proper names only. Identities can be stated with demonstratives and descriptions used in a certain way. But I do concur with Marcus' limitation of L3 to contexts in logical form. I think she is absolutely right in her suggestion that this is how the principle should be understood.

This important restriction allows all the alleged counter-examples to the principle of substitutivity to be circumvented. Consider sentence (3) above. It is false only if understood as expressing the statement made by:

(3*)   Necessarily, there are more than 7 planets.

But if (1) is an identity statement, the phrase 'the number of planets' must be taken to refer to or pick out a particular number—if (1) is true, the number 9. And if (3) is the result of a substitution of one referring expression for a co-referential one into (2), then it cannot be understood as equivalent to (3*). The phrase 'the number of planets' in this use is not eliminable in that way. Thus, correctly understood, if (1) and (2) are true, then so is (3). Once the logical form of (2), and of (3), is clear, the apparent counter-example to the principle of substitutivity disappears.

The intensional counter-example is just as easily handled. Sentence (6) can be false while (4) and (5) are true only if it is taken to make the same statement as:

(6*)   Philip believes that 'Tully denounced Catiline' expresses a true statement.

But if this is an accurate representation of the logical form of (6), then (6) is not a result of the operation of substitution performed on a referential expression in (5). For either (5) will be understood as isomorphic with (6*) and equivalent to

(5*)   Philip believes that 'Cicero denounced Catiline' expresses a true statement.

in which case there is no referential occurrence of 'Cicero' to which the principle can be applied, or it will be understood as of the form

(5′)   Philip believes of Cicero that he denounced Catiline.

in which case there is a referential occurrence of 'Cicero', but an application of substitution based on (4) does not yield a statement of the form of (6*), but rather of the form

(6′)   Philip believes of Tully that he denounced Catiline.

Thus, we have a context in which the principle of substitutivity can be tested relative to the truth of (4) only when we are dealing with (5) and (6′) respectively. And in this context, the principle holds. If (4) and (5′) are true, (6′) is true as well. The possibility that (6*) is false is irrelevant. (6*) is neither necessary nor sufficient for (6′). The principle thus again is vindicated, and can be held as a satisfactory form of Leibniz's Law.

I believe that the force of the different forms of Leibniz's Law, in so far as they are relevant to the epistemic grounding of ordinary identity statements, can be captured in the following formulation, which I shall call simply 'L':

L— Two expressions are co-referential just in case any associated predicate in logical form yields a true statement when attached to one of them if and only if it yields a true statement when attached to the other.

Any utterance or inscription of a sentence intended to express an identity statement makes a true statement if and only if the two referring expressions with which it is made are co-referential. And L presents the necessary and sufficient conditions for co-referentiality. By the phrase 'associated predicate', I mean to restrict the principle to predicates which convey properties in fact thought to characterise the referent of one or the other referring expression. They are predicates 'contained in' the mental file which contains one or the other of those expressions. This restriction of generality, besides being necessary (as Shwayder has suggested, above), is entirely in keeping with my presentation of the principle as an epistemic one. We may take L to be the principle operative in ordinary language for the warranted assertability of identity statements. When it is said that Leibniz's Law governs identity this is what justifiably can be meant. It is on the basis of L that we assess ordinary statements of identity.

Deviant identities

There have been, and are, quite a few philosophers who propound for our acceptance identity statements which seem to stand in obvious violation of Leibniz's Law. The identity claims I have in mind are not of the ordinary garden variety like 'Hesperus is Phosphorus' and 'Cicero is Tully'. They rather constitute, or at least exemplify, quite important metaphysical theses. Often known as 'cross-category identities', they have figured prominently in the phenomenalist and mind-body controversies. They also can appear to crop up in the context of theology. Wherever they occur, they seem to bear significant metaphysical import.

Let me indicate precisely the sort of statements I have in mind. Phenomenalists, at least of the broadly Berkeleyan stripe, characteristically have propounded a general claim that physical objects are identical with collections of sense data. In accordance with this, a phenomenalist will insist of any particular physical object that it is identical with a specific collection of sensa. Likewise, in the philosophy of mind, identity theorists hold that mental states, events or processes are identical with physical (e.g. neural) states, events, or processes. And at the center of Christian theology, providing the foundation for most distinctively Christian beliefs, there is a very remarkable identity which was of great interest to medieval philosophers, the claim that the person who was the man Jesus Christ is one and the same individual as the second person of the divine Trinity, God the Son, a divine being. Unlike the phenomenalist and materialist identities, this striking claim is not an application of a general metaphysical thesis (*pace* Hegel). But like them it seems to link items of categorially heterogeneous status in a way which can appear strictly impossible. Such individuals seem clearly to be essentially and conceptually different in properties, so that no identity statement between them could possibly satisfy the requirements of Leibniz's Law.

I have suggested that Leibniz's Law, appropriately understood, governs our acceptance and rejection of identity statements. It determines their epistemic status, or warranted assertability. Ordinarily, when it is violated, we dismiss the offending statement on that basis. Our decision is relatively simple. But in the case of metaphysically significant cross-category identities, the situation is a bit different. When a phenomenalist, or materialist, or—in the context of Christian theology—a christological identity statement is propounded which seems clearly to fail the test of Leibniz's Law, we hesitate dismissing it outright, or at least we dismiss it only with some degree of uneasiness. For we realise that no such claim is a simple case of mistaken identity, but rather usually stands backed up with an arsenal of arguments which are difficult to assess, and furthermore may embody an attractive metaphysical vision. We thus may begin to wonder about the relation of these statements to Leibniz's Law.

Let us look briefly at some of the relevant features of these cross-category identities, without straying into any details which are not important for our purposes. Consider first mental–physical identities, which have been most widely discussed in recent literature. It has been agreed by many identity theorists as well as their opponents that mental items have properties which neural items cannot even sensibly be said to have, and vice versa. Thoughts, for example, can be cruel or ingenious, puerile or profound. Pains can be throbbing. But surely, many have agreed, it makes no sense to attribute these properties to neuron firings or neural states. A bit of brain matter, or a state it is in, seems conceptually barred from having such properties. Conversely, a neural item can have the property of being located intracranially in region R_1 of the left hemisphere of a brain, a property it would surely make no sense to attribute to my wistful thoughts of Chapel Hill. In short, it seems that on conceptual grounds, mental–physical identity statements cannot possibly satisfy the conditions for truth or warranted assertability specified by Leibniz's Law. And yet in spite of this, they are propounded as true by many scientists and philosophers.

Phenomenalist identities run up against the same difficulty. Physical objects are three dimensional. Sense data, even in collections, are not and cannot be three dimensional. Sense data are essentially private. It is a logical (or conceptual) truth that physical objects are not. And so forth. So again, Leibniz's Law is violated in the most flagrant way.

Consider finally that identity claim foundational for orthodox Christian theology, the claim that Jesus was God the Son. In traditional thought, God has such properties as omnipresence and necessary sinlessness, as well as aseity, eternality, and immutability, properties which surely it seems could not possibly characterise a particular man. Likewise, Jesus was born of Jewish parentage and died a death by execution, properties which God appears conceptually barred from having.

In each case, we have an identity claim, or set of such claims, which a number of intelligent philosophers have espoused as important metaphysical truths. Yet these claims seem to stand in obvious violation of Leibniz's Law. A cross-category identity statement will not satisfy the requirements of L, as I have sketched it out above. For the notion of a logical or conceptual category is such that referring expressions in two different categories logically cannot have all the same predicates meaningfully attached to them. And a cross-category identity is constructed with referring expressions from two distinct categories.

How, then, should we think of the relation of such statements to Leibniz's Law? Should their existence cause us to doubt the alleged role of L in the assessing of identity statements? Serious doubt can be thrown on Leibniz's Law by the existence of apparently cross-category identities. For it is not the case that all identities widely thought to be of this type are such esoteric metaphysical theses as the controversial examples just mentioned. Some are undeniably true, or at least as warrantedly assertable as anything in science. Consider, for instance, the identification of temperature with mean kinetic energy. On the basis of this general theoretical identity, the specific temperature of any body will be identified with the mean kinetic energy of its molecular constitution. But such identities have seemed to many philosophers to be clearly cross-category. An example the late James Cornman used to discuss a lot involves the fact that the temperature of a body can have, for instance, the property of being 27° centigrade, a property which is not meaningfully ascribable to the mean kinetic energy of that body's molecules. Many, if not all, of the theoretical identities in science will issue in this sort of divergence in predications. Thomas Nagel, for his part, tells us that his being kicked by a horse can be ridiculous, although the vastly complex molecular event with which the kick is identical can hardly be properly so characterised. But surely, we do not allow such violations of Leibniz's Law to cast a shadow of doubt on these identities yielded by modern science.

Many other alleged examples of identities which are clearly true and yet stand in violation of L have been offered in recent literature. Alan White has claimed that a piece of paper, suitably inscribed, can *be* a contract. Yet the contract can have the properties of having been hotly debated and finally agreed to, being harsh for one party, and being legally binding— properties no piece of paper meaningfully can be said to have. Likewise, the paper can be vellum and quarto, properties not meaningfully ascribed to contracts. White also offers the example of an actor *being* Hamlet. Yet, while it is true that Hamlet is played by many actors, it is not true or even meaningful to say of the particular actor who is Hamlet that he is played by many actors. With this compare the factual truth that Ronald Reagan is now one and the same individual as the President of the United States. The President is elected every four years. And, surprisingly successful as he may be, it is not true of Ronald Reagan that he is elected every four years.

One final example may be of interest. Consider a game of chess underway, played with wooden chessmen. It can be true to say 'This piece of wood is the black king'. And yet, although it is true that the black king could have been ivory, granite, or plastic, it is necessarily false that the piece of wood could have been ivory, granite, or plastic. It could be true that this wood carving was done yesterday, and so came into existence yesterday. It is false that the black king came into existence then, having on the contrary existed as a piece in the game of chess since its inception in its present form.

These examples are in some ways a heterogeneous lot. They are the sorts of statements often presented as identities, as true, and yet as standing in violation of Leibniz's Law. They can give us serious pause, to say the least, over any identity principle which would rule them out, one and all.

It should be clear that our assessment of any genuinely cross-category identity, if it is based on the understanding of Leibniz's Law presented in the chapter, will be the same. We shall judge that no such statement is warrantedly assertible. And in so far as decisions of warranted assertibility are connected with assessments of truth value, it seems we must judge them all false. Further, in any case where Leibniz's Law could not possibility or even meaningfully be satisfied, we shall judge the offending statement to be necessarily—logically or conceptually—false, if meaningful at all. Obviously, then, we have here a philosophical problem of some interest concerning identity statements and Leibniz's Law.

As a first step toward dealing with this problem, let us review briefly our range of examples purporting to be true identities which violate Leibniz's Law (rendering each in a form of the same level of generality, and using lower case letters as rigid designators):

(1)   Mental item *m* is neural item *n*.
(2)   Physical object *p* is collection of sensa *s*.
(3)   Jesus of Nazareth is God the Son.
(4)   The temperature of *b* is the mean kinetic molecular energy of *b*.
(5)   Nagel's being kicked is the complex molecular event *e*.
(6)   This piece of paper is the contract.
(7)   This actor is Hamlet.
(8)   Ronald Reagan is the President of the US.
(9)   This piece of wood is the black king.

Examples (6)–(9) are easily dealt with. In each case, we have on the LHS (left hand side) of the sentence a designation of some individual, and on the RHS, something like a title term, the name of some role that individual plays, or some conventional status it has within an institutional context, created and governed by constitutive rules which are definitive of that role or status. The LHS picks out the individual with common referential devices. The RHS employs title-designational devices peculiar to, and operative only within, the special rule-governed context.

Sentences such as (6)–(9) are rarely used to express literal statements of numerical identity. Employing title terms, they most often would be used to convey predications, in which case Leibniz's Law is not directly relevant. Sentence (8) alone is likely to be used on occasion to express an identity statement. And it is not at all clearly cross-category in status. Apparent violations of L such as that mentioned above with the predicate 'is elected every four years' are generated illegitimately by switching the semantic role of the definite description on the RHS (compare with this the alleged failures of substitutivity discussed in the last section). When the description retains the function it must have to be used in an identity statement, no violations of L arise. Should sentences such as (6), (7) and (9) ever be used to express anything like identity statements, it is possible to retain their truth only if they are viewed as metaphorical identities, a category of usage to be spelled out at the end of chapter eight. They will then be context relative identities, satisfying L within the bounds and interests of the relevant context. I can see no deep philosophical problems raised by (6)–(9), and no serious challenge to the claims I have made about Leibniz's Law governing identity statements.

Sentences (1)–(5) are a different matter. (4) and (5) present examples of what we may call 'micro-identities', identity statements whose LHS pick out some phenomenal physical object or substance with ordinary, non-technical referring expressions, and whose RHS employ technical terms of one of the natural sciences which designate by reference to microstructures, molecular, atomic and sub-atomic entities, and the like. Some philosophers

have viewed micro-identities as equivalence relations 'weaker than numerical identity', as they often have put it. May Brodbeck and Thomas
Nagel have at some time taken this approach. On this view, nothing about
micro-identities can cast any doubt on Leibniz's Law, as it governs only
statements of strict numerical identity.

But this has not been found by many philosophers to be a very attractive
view. Micro-identities are treated by most as literal statements of numerical
identity. Consequently, the differences between the two terms in the LHS
and RHS of such statements have given rise to stubborn metaphysical
questions, some of which have been focused in the discussion of the
problem of Eddington's 'two tables', and more generally, under the rubric
of 'scientific realism'. Understood as strict, numerical identities, micro-
identities enter the ranks of (1)–(3) as propositions which either are
themselves of significant metaphysical interest, or at least exemplify general
theses of such interest.

The physicalist, phenomenalist, christological, and micro-identity statements represented by (1)–(5) appear to be cross-category and thus to
conflict with Leibniz's Law, as stated. When challenged with Leibniz's
Law, the proponent of such a claim as a literal statement of numerical
identity has a number of possible options available to him. Of course, he
could acknowledge that he is wrong and retract his claim. But this rarely if
ever is done. The theoretical (metaphysical or theological) motivations
behind such a claim are too strong to allow it so easily to be defeated.
Another possible move is to deny the governance of Leibniz's Law over
identity statements at all. But this is philosophically problematic in the
extreme. As David Wiggins has put it:[16]

> If Leibniz's Law is dropped . . . then we need some formal principle or other, and
> one of at least comparable university, to justify the valid instances of the
> intersubstitution of identicals.

And what would such a principle be? Moreover, any allegation that
identity statements are not in any sense governed by Leibniz's Law just
seems to be false.

Acknowledging the role of Leibniz's Law, our metaphysician or
theologian could claim that a proper understanding of the properties of the
object x and the object y identified will show that the violation is not real,
but apparent only. Concerning displayed sentence (4) above, for example,
the identification of temperature with mean kinetic energy, it could be
argued that when all associated predicates of the two singular terms are put
in proper logical form, no genuine violations of Leibniz's Law remain. The
predicate 'is 27° centigrade' would then become something like 'registers

27° centigrade on a standard instrument of such-and-such a type'. And this would be held to be as true of the RHS as of the LHS of (4). Likewise, the theologian could reconsider and rework his construal of divine and human properties in such a way that no incompatibility arises. It is my opinion that this is how the christological identity claims in fact ought to be dealt with. They ought not to be understood as cross-category identities at all. This suggestion, and this general stragegy will be developed in chapter nine. The point now is that not all philosophers and theologians have been prepared to take this tack. And that is because this kind of move is generally thought not to be very plausible. If sense data, material objects, clouds of micro-particles, mental entities, and divine beings, etc. are all such as to be the bearers of properties, it can seem quite clear that their properties will be *so* different in kind, so categorically different, as to be *totally* unshareable. No one entity could be literally characterised by properties of more than one such category.

One other strategy is available. It has attained some popularity in the controversy over the mind-body problem. This move involves a recognition of Leibniz's Law, and an acknowledgement of the very different predicates which are attachable to the subject and predicate nominative terms of any cross-category identity to form true statements. It consists in the attempt to amend or re-formulate Leibniz's Law so that it allows for the particular failures of substitution which attend such identities. If the suggestion of emendation is no more than a merely *ad hoc* device to save a favoured position, it can be thought to be no more plausible or interesting than the other possible moves. But it can be presented as legitimated by some trends of philosophical thought which have attained prominence in the past half-century. The metaphysician can argue that some quite general considerations about the conceptual multiplicity of natural languages underly the need to re-formulate Leibniz's Law. Consequently, this strategy can seem quite attractive.

If there is any justification for the assertion and acceptance of genuinely and ultimately deviant identity statements, it will be some version of this move. In the next chapter, I shall construct in general form the kind of theory which alone would allow this move to work, and thus provide for the possibility of a positive assessment of any deviant metaphysical identities. Then, in the following chapter, I shall evaluate the theory. We shall see whether any identity statements can escape the net of Leibniz's Law, as traditionally conceived, and thus require our assessment on some other basis.

7

The Theory of Regulative
Identity

It has been suggested that Leibniz's Law, appropriately understood, governs the warranted assertability of identity statements. But a range of identity statements has been brought to our attention whose members can seem clearly to violate Leibniz's Law in any of its traditional formulations, and yet are held by many philosophers to bear important metaphysical truth. These are statements commonly known as 'cross-category identities', and have figured centrally in a few well known metaphysical and theological positions. I have suggested that one interesting move available to a proponent of such identities when challenged with Leibniz's Law is to make a two-fold claim on some general grounds that Leibniz's Law needs to be reformulated, and further that the resulting formulation will allow the truth of these statements.

It is important for our understanding of the epistemic status of identity statements, of how their truth value is assessed, that we examine this claim. So in this chapter, I shall present a general line of argument concerning human conceptualisation and language which alone might legitimate a reformulation of Leibniz's Law that would allow for the truth of cross-category identities.

For reasons to be stated later, I shall refer to the general apparatus underlying and encompassing the reformulated law as 'the theory of regulative identity'. I develop this theory for the most part independently of parallel arguments and notions in recent literature so that its broad outlines can be made clear and will not be obscured with what, in this context, would be unnecessary detail. For this reason, I do not discuss particular emendations of Leibniz's Law similar to that to be developed here which have been presented in the specific context of the mind-body identity controversy.[1] Likewise, I drop the notion of a 'category' and avoid that of a logical 'type', adverting to a more general notion which will serve the same

function in the theory as one of these would, without involving commitment to a controversial position on such widely discussed and notoriously
difficult notions. The theory of regulative identity developed in this chapter
then will be evaluated in the next.

Modes of discourse

A philosophical understanding of human language to some extent
predominant in the first half of this century saw it as dependent upon a
single uniform logical structure for its fact stating capabilities. A *locus
classicus* for this view is of course Wittgenstein's *Tractatus*. Attempting to
account for the ability of scientific as well as ordinary language to refer to
the world, Wittgenstein purported to identify a uniform and pervasive
logical form underlying all factual statement. Conformity with such a
comprehensive structure was then seen by many philosophers to be a
condition, or *the* condition, for language being used meaningfully or
intelligibly. The *Tractatus* embodied an intellectual vision, a sort of
philosophico-linguistic aesthetic, which was shared by many philosophers,
even those who dissented from Wittgenstein's opinion that ordinary
language in fact has such a substructure. These dissenters engaged in a
quest for an ideal constructed language which *would* conform to such a
single logical pattern. But whether or not they thought ordinary natural
languages in fact have a uniform substructure, the majority of the most
prominent philosophers of the time agreed that any language fit for
determinate factual statement must have such a form.

We might say that in such an ideal representation of language, all its
parts stand in clear logical relation to all its other parts. Take any referring
expression, couple with it any predicate expression according to the
relevant rules of syntax for declarative sentences, and you will have (either
simpliciter, or as uttered by a speaker of the language) a statement of
determinate truth value: true or false. But then over a period of time, and
for various reasons (including reflection over some troubling paradoxes),
some philosophers came to realise that there are important differences
between kinds of referring expression and kinds of predicate such that not
just any grammatically well-formed subject-predicate sentence makes a
logically proper statement. At first this realisation was still tied to the old
image of language. All fact stating language was still thought to be cut from
one logical cloth, although the weave was recognised to be less smooth, a
little knobbier and more complex, than had been assumed.

Of course, it was realised that we can talk about quite different *kinds* of
things. We can talk about material objects, our own perceptions and
sensations, persons, energy fields, theoretical entities, and abstract objects,

among other things. We can also make aesthetic, ethical, and religious remarks. Many adherents of the logical uniformity view of language relegated these last kinds of remark to a realm of the nonfactual, as not standing in clear logical relation to paradigmatically factual statements, such as those made in the physical sciences. All factual statements were thought to bear standard logical relations to one another, across their apparent boundaries of subject matter. For example, the main-line phenomenalist enterprise held that normal logical relations of entailment, equivalence, and contradiction obtain between statements taken singly or in groups from the range of material object statements and that of sense datum statements. The analytical phenomenalist claim was that material object statements are equivalent to, and thus can be analysed into, sense datum statements. Another philosophical movement, logical behaviourism, held that certain statements about persons, psychological statements, could be analysed into material object statements in a similar manner. So language, in spite of its obvious surface variegation, still was held to be, in its depth, of a uniform logical structure.

But then, from some insights of Wittgenstein's later work, among other sources, it came to be realised that human language encompasses much more real and significant diversity than had been imagined. To be fact stating, language does not have to conform to some one simple logical structure; rather, it is the various structuring of language which determines what is to count as 'fact' in any of a wide range of human concerns. It came to be thought by some that the structures of language, and the corresponding structures of the world that we present to ourselves through language, are a function of human interests, and thus are determined by language users.

One of the first writers to apply such perspectives as these was Friedrich Waismann. He repeatedly claimed in print that within the scope of assertive language use there is discernible a multiplicity of what he called 'language strata'. According to him, a stratum of language is constituted by a kind of statement, identifiable by broadly logical means. As examples of kinds of statements making up different language strata, he offered:[2]

> laws of nature, material object statements, sense datum statements, statements describing a dream, a blurred memory picture, sentences which occur in a novel, and so on . . . a psychological statement . . . a geometrical proposition, a statement describing national characteristics. . . .

Waismann actually did not go very far in delimiting strata in a detailed and precise way. He introduced the notion of such a division within language use by means of examples such as those above, and by explaining how such different kinds of statement differ not just in subject matter but in logic.

For example, he suggested that only within certain strata is completeness of description possible. Within the language of geometry, a triangle can be described completely. But material object language is such that no finality of description is possible. He also suggested that such fundamental concepts as truth might be systematically ambiguous between strata, finding their use differently in those different linguistic contexts. And, most importantly, he maintained that the traditional laws of logic hold only within, and not between different strata, some actually failing to hold within certain strata. In summary, he says:[3]

> Thus we see that statements may be *true* in different senses; that they may be *verifiable* in different senses; that they may be *complete* or *incomplete* in different senses; indeed that logic itself may vary with the sort of statement. This suggests grouping in the same stratum all those sentences which are homogenous, i.e., which logically behave in the same way.

Having drawn these distinctions between language strata, Waismann went on to claim that it is the relations *between* strata, which are of most philosophical interest. He suggested that many of the central problems of philosophy arise at their points of meeting. As examples he gave 'the problem of perception, of verification, of induction, the problem of the relation between mind and body'. The analytical phenomenalist program was doomed to fail because of the logical differences between sense datum statements and material object statements, and the absence of simple logical relations between the two strata. The same was true of logical behaviourism. Overall, Waismann maintained that:[4]

> So long as we move only among the statements of a single stratum, all the relations provided by logic remain valid. The real problem arises where two strata make contact, so to speak; it is the problem of these planes of contact which today should claim the attention of the logician.

At this point, I would like to introduce a terminological change. The term 'strata' easily carries connotations of a simple hierarchy or stratification among the linguistic divisions so designated. In order to avoid this implication, or association, I shall use the phrase 'modes of discourse'. Following Waismann, let us suppose that there are discernible within the range of factual human language use various modes of discourse, identifiable in a broadly logical way. But, enlarging on his remarks, let us specify the content of a mode of discourse in a slightly different way. We shall view a mode of discourse not as composed of, or constituted by, a kind of statement, but as consisting of those linguistic items and habits allowing for the making of a certain kind of statement. By linguistic items I do not mean grammatical items such as nouns, adjectives, and so forth, or syntactical items such as subjects and verbs, but such things as concepts, referential expressions, and predicates.

The use of language is a human activity. A mode of discourse is a mode of that activity. A particular linguistic act, if it communicates at all, or serves any peculiarly linguistic function, does so always and only as it takes place within a particular mode of discourse. It is the logical, referential, and general expressive wherewithal of that mode of discourse which makes any such act possible. For example, my ability to talk about Waismann, as distinct from his positions, depends on the stock, structure, and powers of what may be called the human, or more generally, the personal, mode of discourse. I depend on a way of referring to him, which means I depend on conventions involving proper names and individuation. These ways of referring depend on contained or associated sortal concepts. And associated with these concepts, along with the appropriate referring expressions, are all those predicates which, taken together with the roles, skills, or habits of their proper employment, make up a mode of discourse.

There are many and interesting interrelations between modes of discourse logically distinguishable. Take for example two of the 'strata' Waismann identifies: scientific laws and material object statements. Clearly, lower order scientific generalisations operate in many cases with the same concepts as particular material object statements. At what point of increasing generality or theory-ladenness is a mode of discourse distinct from that containing ordinary material object statements reached? Again, consider what we might call the physical mode of discourse (material object statements) and the human or personal mode of discourse (psychological statements, ascriptions of agency, etc.). An interesting case can be made that statements in the latter mode of discourse depend logically on the former. Strawson, for instance, has argued that individuation depends on a unified framework of spatio-temporal relations; thus, talk of persons would depend logically on being able to talk of their bodies.[5] And other sorts of arguments for the same conclusion can be formulated. If this is the case, then it may well be that the physical mode of discourse is at least in some ways more fundamental in our overall scheme of language and thought than the personal mode of discourse.

In fact, it could be argued that this mode of discourse serves as logical foundation for all the rest. Talk of sense data, scientific laws and theoretical entities, talk about persons, abstraction, and all the rest arise out of our contact with the physical world. This is where they all have their logical roots. It is the variegated nature of our experience of the physical world which gives rise to our developing different modes of discourse. And it is through these different ways of talking about the world that we are able to satisfy our diverse interests. Different kinds of knowledge, different kinds of understanding are yielded by these logically different modes of dividing up the world for thought, comment, and action. Ontologically, we live in one world, although conceptually we live in many.

Modes of discourse and identity statements

The relevance of all this for an understanding of identity statements should now be indicated. The kind of identity statement most commonly made has both its referring expressions drawn from the same mode of discourse. The claim that Cicero is Tully is an identity statement made within the human mode of discourse. 'Cicero' is a proper name for a human being. So is 'Tully'. By an utterance of 'Cicero is Tully', we are informed that, among other things, one individual man is called by both names. Built into the human mode of discourse, one might say, are ways of individuating one man from another. As the sortal associated with, or backing up, the use of these proper names, 'man' is a count noun. And it is the kind of count noun for which at least rough and practical principles for individuation, re-identification, and counting can be supplied. There are ways of determining from the descriptive information associated with 'Cicero' and that associated with 'Tully' whether, in a certain context of their use, they name one or two individuals. The identity statement made with them presents them as referring to only one man. And it is by applying Leibniz's Law to this claim that we ascertain its truth value, or at least determine whether it is warrantedly assertable. Leibniz's Law thus provides the epistemic grounding for this ordinary kind of identity statement.

The two names 'Cicero' and 'Tully' come from the same mode of discourse, or customarily find their use in the same mode of discourse. So do the two names in the sentence 'Hesperus is Phosphorus', but it is a physical mode of discourse. Two referring expressions from the same mode of discourse have their place in the same logical nexus. They are logically and conceptually related. Thus, there is nothing logically odd about their being used together in an identity statement. With sufficient information available, a straightforward application of Leibniz's Law can (in principle) show whether or not they are co-referential. There are, embedded in their common mode of discourse and associated with the sortal under which they are used, criteria for individuation and counting sufficient in principal to adjudicate the question as to whether they are being used to name one and the same object, or two different ones. They are co-referential just in case each of the relevant predicates true of one is true of the other. It is that simple.

But let us consider a different sort of case. Our account of a multiplicity of modes of discourse within language, each containing such linguistic equipment as referential expressions, leaves open the possibility of an identity statement being made whose two referring expressions are drawn from two different modes of discourse. Every informative identity statement presents us with one object as referred to in two different ways. Such an identity statement would present two very different, logically different, ways of talking as being ways of talking about one and the same object. We could say that it is an identity statement made between modes of discourse, or that it 'bridges' modes of discourse.

Clear examples of such identity statements have not in the past been as common as they are today. Our various modes of discourse traditionally have been understood in such a way that they were thought to be ways of talking about different kinds of objects, not different ways of talking about the same objects. The conceptual multiplicity has long been thought to have been generated by our recognition of an ontological multiplicity, to which it corresponds.[6]

The realisation of some philosophers that talk about our sense impressions is interestingly different from talk about material objects led in some cases to a reification of sense data as particulars ontologically distinct from material, or physical, particulars. And the existence of the personal mode of discourse has long led philosophers, theologians, and laymen to reify its major category of referents, souls or minds, as ontologically distinct from physical bodies. Yet more recent trends of thought in science and philosophy have led to a reversal of this tendency toward ontological multiplication. Increasingly, it has come to be thought that the personal mode of discourse is a way of talking about living organisms of a certain kind as they are complexly related to, and are in interaction with, their environment. In this mode of discourse it is not immaterial individuals which are referred to, but rather living material objects which are referred to in a logically distinct way. Logical, epistemological, and scientific problems have been seen to attend the view of a dualist ontology corresponding to the two distinct modes of discourse, personal and physical. And likewise, such problems have been found to undermine and render unnecessary, if not just unintelligible, the separation of sense data from physical objects as entities ontologically distinct. Nor, finally, is Eddington's dualistic postulation of 'two tables' countenanced by many at all. So the stage now is set, it might seem, for asserting identity statements between such modes of discourse.

An identity always has a certain reductive ontological import. Whereas we might have thought that the two referring expressions with which it is made referred to two different objects, the assertion of the identity statement presents them as co-referential, referring only to one. This is the import of every identity statement made within a mode of discourse; and if they can be made between modes of discourse, it will be their import as well. So if our various modes of discourse are in fact different ways of talking about one and the same world, it seems that identity statements between them might be used to indicate this in particular cases. Such an identity statement would present its two referring expressions not as ways of referring to two different objects of two different sorts, but as two ways of referring to one and the same object.

Let us try to construct a simple, concrete example of such an identity statement. Consider the sentence 'That is Tom Morris'. As uttered by a speaker of English while pointing toward a certain physical object, the appropriate human body, it might be taken to convey such an identity statement. 'Tom Morris' is a proper name having its use within the human, or personal, mode of discourse. 'That', as part of the particular ostensive act, does not serve to pick out an immaterial object, such as a soul, identified by the statement as Tom Morris. It seems rather to indicate a perceptible body, a physical object. If it does, then the statement made with this sentence can be taken to be an identity statement between modes of discourse.

But it is arguable that the reference of 'that' depends on the sortal backing up the use of 'Tom Morris'. This sortal is part of the personal mode of discourse, and thus this use of the demonstrative must be assigned to that mode of discourse as well. Demonstratives are available in every mode of discourse admitting of individuation and reference. And every particular standardly communicative use of a demonstrative depends, on that occasion of its use, on some sortal deriving from one particular mode of discourse. If an utterance of the above sentence makes an identity statement, and the demonstrative is used within the personal mode of discourse, then the statement made is a standard, or ordinary, identity statement made within a single mode of discourse. Furthermore, since it is even arguable that this sentence makes no identity statement at all, we shall try another example.

Consider the following sentence:

T— Tom Morris is just this physical organism with all its complex processes and environmental interactions.

On a given occasion of its use by an English speaker, T could be used to make a cross-mode identity statement, one between modes of discourse. It would be a characteristic claim for a physicalist or materialist to make. The word 'just' is unnecessary, but customarily serves to underline the reductive ontological import of such a statement. An assertion made by the use of a sentence such as T would be in effect a denial that the person named is anything (ontologically) more or other than the particular complex physical object designated.

Traditionally, it has been alleged against such statements, and has been a thorn in the flesh for proponents of materialist positions, that they violate Leibniz's Law and are therefore false. More strongly, it is claimed that application of Leibniz's Law shows that they *could* not be true. Predicates truly affirmed of one of the terms are not truly affirmable of the other. For example, physical items—bodies, events, processes—have more or less exact spatial location. But, it is alleged, this is not true of mental items. Joining a spatial predicate to a subject denoting a mental item generates a meaningless string of words, or at best a conceptually false statement, something that could not possibly be true. How could an immaterial particular, it is asked, have a spatial property? And, of course, it is also claimed that mental particulars have properties which could not possibly be had by physical objects. On this basis, it is concluded that no identity statement which draws its two referring expressions from the personal and physical modes of discourse, one from each, can possibly be true. For example, it is said by those who find this argument compelling that no thought or sensation could be identical with a neural event or process. The neural particular would have a spatial location; but it would be meaningless to say of a thought that it was located, for instance, two inches behind the bridge of someone's nose. And conversely, the thought might be a valid argument, something no neural item could be said, meaningfully, to be. The violations of Leibniz's Law preclude the warranted assertion of any identity statement between items of two such distinct modes of discourse. So the argument goes.[7]

It is important to note, however, about such cases that all the apparent violations of Leibniz's Law are of a certain interesting type. A predicate which, when attached to one referring expression, yields a true statement, joined to the other is thought to yield either no meaningful statement at all, or one which is logically or conceptually false, necessarily false due to semantic deviance, and so true under no possible circumstances.[8] It is never the case in one of these instances of violation that a predicate empirically, or contingently, true of the one is seen as empirically, contingently, or non-deviantly false of the other. It is, on this view, not empirically, or even straightforwardly, false that my pleasure in writing this occupies a cubic millimetre two and a quarter inches behind the bridge of my nose; such a claim is seen as being rather without determinate content. It is held that there are not procedures for deciding the question, given the way the relevant concepts are related.

So there are apparently two distinct ways in which the traditionally formulated principles of Leibniz's Law can be violated. There are the cases in which predicates true of one of the purportedly co-referential expressions is meaningfully (non-deviantly) false of the other. And there are the cases of identities between modes of discourse, in regard to whose referring expressions a predicate true of one may not be meaningfully applicable to the other, or a predicate empirically or contingently true of one may be logically (conceptually) false of the other. The important question which arises at this point is whether, in light of the view of language as containing multiple modes of discourse, Leibniz's Law should be so formulated and understood that it precludes the truth, or warranted assertion, of any and every cross-mode identity statement.

As I have mentioned already, there is a strong tendency in contemporary thought to construe our various modes of discourse as logically distinct ways of talking about one world. Our conceptual multiplicity is not taken to imply a corresponding ontological multiplicity. Should the logical boundaries between modes of discourse, the logical differences between them, disallow our indicating this in particular cases by means of identity statements? Referring expressions in a given mode of discourse will have their use in a particular conceptual and logical nexus, and will have applicable to them a range of predicates endemic to that mode and circumscribed by its boundaries. So we should expect misfires when attempting to join a predicate drawn from one mode to a referring expression otherwise derived.[9] But should this debar us from employing the reductive force of identity statements to indicate a relation between the modes? It is at least not utterly obvious that it should. Thus, it may be wise to consider an emendation of Leibniz's Law consonant with this new view of language.

The precise statement of an emended version of Leibniz's Law will depend on whether we consider cross-mode predications (the result of attaching a predicate drawn from one mode to a referring expression drawn from a different one) to be strictly meaningless sentences, or to make statements which are necessarily (logically or conceptually) false. If we take the first option, we can rewrite L in this way:

L'—Two expressions are co-referential just in case any associated predicate in logical form yields a true statement when attached to one if and only if it does not yield a false statement when attached to the other.

The emendation involves an alteration of only the last clause of L. This version of the law does not require that every relevant predicate true of one of two co-referential expressions be true of the other, only that it not be false of the other.

If we take cross-mode predications to yield necessarily (conceptually) false statements a different version is needed:

> L″—Two expressions are co-referential just in case any associated predicate in logical form which yields an empirically or contigently true statement when attached to one does not yield an empirically or contingently false statement when attached to the other.

The one limitation on L″ is that it can govern only empirical identity statements. By 'empirical identity statement', I mean roughly any identity statement made by the utterance of a sentence whose contained referring expressions refer to empirical objects. And, in turn, an empirical object is any object such that some non-intensional predicates true of it are empirically, or contingently, not necessarily or analytically, true of it. On this definition of empirical identity statements, such a statement is made by a standard use of 'Cicero is Tully' but *not* by '9 is the number of the planets' or '4 is the square of 2'. As long as the cross-mode identities are treated as empirical identity statements, either version could be taken to serve our purposes. Both versions allow the possibility of cross-mode identity statements. In the case of materialist identities, the spatial predicates true of any neural item are either not false or not contingently, empirically false of any mental item. Thus, the materialist identities are not ruled out by Leibniz's Law in its new versions.

Constitutive and regulative identities

At this point I shall introduce a terminological distinction between identity statements made within a mode of discourse, and those made between two different modes. The former I shall call 'constitutive identity statements', the latter, 'regulative identity statements'. The descriptive terms 'regulative' and 'constitutive' are chosen to indicate the difference in logical and epistemic status of the two types of statement. Briefly, the truth, or warranted assertability, of a constitutive identity statement is ascertained (ultimately) by means of an application of Leibniz's Law. Because of this, beliefs concerning constitutive identity statements can be said under the appropriate circumstances to constitute in a clear sense knowledge. There are intersubjectively available and applicable decision procedures for determining the truth value of such a statement. Both of its referring expressions pick out their referent by means of the same conceptuality, or by means of the wherewithal of the same mode of discourse. Every relevant predicate true of one will be true of the other, if they are in fact co-referential. But let us look at the quite different case of regulative identities.

Any identity statement purports to be about one object; it purports to present to our attention one object. This is true of regulative as well as constitutive identities. But we may say that a regulative identity statement presents two quite different logical subjects as appearances of only one ontological subject. A logical subject is to be understood as the intensional referent of a referring expression or set of co-referential expressions as used within a mode of discourse, which can be individuated and described by and only by the conceptual means of that particular mode. An ontological subject is an entity which exists in some fundamental sense, as a basic part of the furniture of the universe. Its existence is necessary but not sufficient for the existence of one or more logical subjects by means of which we are epistemically related to it. The traditional understanding of language whose rejection is required by the theory under development here holds logical and ontological subjects to exist in one-to-one correspondence, or more accurately, to coincide. If our talk of minds is distinct from our talk of bodies, then among the furniture of the universe are both minds and bodies. But a rejection of this position which holds out the possibility that multiple logical subjects correspond to one ontological subject will allow that it is not necessary for the truth of a regulative identity statement that all relevant predicates from one of the involved modes satisfied by one of the logical subjects be true also of the referring expression from the other mode. So the truth of a regulative identity statement is not quite so simple a matter. It is possible, and even to be expected, that many of the predicates true of one of such a pair of co-referential expressions will not be true of the other, either because they are not meaningfully predicable of it, or are logically false of it. Indeed, the question is: Will there be *any* predicates true of both? More specifically, will there be any non-modal, non-intensional predicates (ruling out such 'high' predicates as 'interesting') true of both? If the two referring terms come from two completely distinct modes of discourse, each having its own logical and conceptual nexus with its own range of predicates, then how can we expect *any* such predicate to apply to both? And without this expectation, without the possibility of affirming any of the same such predicates of two such different terms, on what grounds would we ever be led to hold that they are co-referential? How could this kind of identity statement in any way be warrantedly asserted?

There are at least two possible approaches to this problem. One is to make the constitutive-regulative distinction context relative. A particular statement could be regulative relative to the two modes of discourse it bridges, but constitutive relative to a third, over-arching mode, comprehending within its scope the entirety, or at least the relevant parts, of the other two. This is a move akin to one employed by Nagel in 'Physicalism'. In the case of many alleged cross-category identities, this might be a difficult claim to make out. A variation of this approach would be the claim that modes of discourse need not be completely distinct. They may overlap, or have concepts and predicates in common. In either case, there would be available predicates meaningfully applicable to both referring expressions, by means of which some backing or warrant could be supplied for the presentation of them as co-referential. It would be applications of a reformulated version of Leibniz's Law in regard to these predicates which would ground the truth claim being made.

There is, however, a quite different approach to the question of how the truth of a regulative identity statement is ascertained, warranted, or grounded. Suppose our modes of discourse are distinct, and there are no non-modal, non-intensional predicates applicable to both of any two referential expressions taken from two different modes. It might be suggested that the very existence of different modes of discourse is due to a desire to capture and explain a significant variety in the kinds of experience had by human beings. And it is thus experience which links them.

The most common kind of human experience has given rise to the physical mode of discourse, which encompasses the conception of an external world of three dimensional material objects existing through time. A kind of experience almost as common has given rise to the personal mode of discourse. That is, the nature of the experience of certain kinds of three dimensional material objects could not be captured or sufficiently articulated in the physical mode of discourse. Thus arose the personal mode, with the conceptual wherewithal adequate for this distinct, supervenient experience.

With regard to our experience of persons, we might say that physical object language does not go far enough. But for another range of experience, it goes too far. Thus arose (at least among philosophers) what we might call the perceptual, the sense-datum, mode of discourse. And again, in some cases a kind of experience is had for which none of these modes is felt to offer sufficient powers of articulation. The personal mode comes closest, but does not go far enough. So there has arisen what can be referred to as the divine mode of discourse, or God-talk.

In a somewhat different but related vein, the theoretical discourse of the sciences has arisen in an effort to describe and explain as accurately and comprehensively as possible certain ranges of our experience and its objects. So each of these modes of discourse somehow is rooted firmly in human experience. And it is experience which connects them. For all its problems, phenomenalism tried to spell out how it is that when we experience a certain range of sense data, we experience material objects, and vice versa. And for all their problems, the logical behaviorists, central state materialists, and other mind-body identity theorists have been trying to spell out the fact that when we experience certain physical objects in certain ways, we experience persons, and vice versa. It is thus a complex function of experience which leads us to talk of a particular physical object when confronted with particular sense data, or to talk of a particular person when perceiving a particular physical object.

It may thus be experience which in some way grounds any regulative identity statement, which gives rise to its utterance, and against which its truth is checked. But 'checked' is here a somewhat misleading term. If this is how regulative identity statements are grounded, it is much different from the grounding of other identities. It is not the intersubjectively possible application of a simple principle which grounds them, but rather general constraints on accounting for or explaining an experience or range of experience. Of course, by 'experience' is not meant *sense* experience, but some broader and more comprehensive notion. It also could be suggested that it is rather some sort of metaphysical insight or intuition arising out of, or at least illuminating, the relevant experience which grounds and thus warrants these identities. And if this is the case, there can be no proof of their truth or falsity. They cannot be said to constitute knowledge in the way that an identity statement made *within* a mode of discourse can. But in so far as they are held to be true, they serve to regulate the way in which their two involved modes of discourse are related. This is the reason for their appellation.

There is a great deal of vagueness to what has just been said. But I do not see how any comments of sufficient generality on this point can be made much more determinate or precise. From what has been said, it should be clear that the lack of a simple logical apparatus, or a clear cut principle, for ascertaining the truth of a regulative identity statement would allow room for intersubjective disagreement not allowed in the case of an ordinary constitutive identity. And it is interesting to note that general positions regarding the truth value of identities between modes of discourse are often paradigms of endlessly controversial metaphysical positions. The lack of any simple or straightforward principles by which to settle questions concerning the interrelations of modes of discourse and the coincidence or otherwise of their referents goes at least some way toward accounting for the intractability of such metaphysical disputes.

So the emended version of Leibniz's Law, it can be argued, grounds the most familiar kind of identity statement, the constitutive identity, and *allows* for the truth of that (relatively) rare kind of identity statement, the regulative identity. If such an understanding of Leibniz's Law and the epistemic status of identity statements is acceptable, and *only* if it is acceptable, will it be possible that any of the well known and controversial 'cross-category identities' can true identity statements as well as being genuinely cross-category. They will have to be seen as of this regulative variety.

8

Metaphysical and Metaphorical Identities

The theory of regulative identity just presented in broad outline suggests that a fairly recent perspective on the conceptual complexity of natural languages allows for a new understanding of Leibniz's Law, according to which it is possible to have true identity statements which bridge quite diverse, logically diverse, ways of talking about the world. If the theory is acceptable, then it may be that only a restricted, or suitably reformulated version of Leibniz's Law, such as one of those presented in the last chapter, properly governs our assessment of identity statements. And in that case, some significant and controversial metaphysical identities (e.g. phenomenalist, materialist, christological) which have been widely thought to violate it in its traditional forms, may escape its net and call for our acceptance or rejection on some other basis.

In this chapter, I want to sketch out several difficulties the theory faces, none of which may be an obviously insurmountable obstacle for it, but some of which tell very seriously against it. These difficulties will be sufficiently general to apply to any version of such a theory which might be developed. None of them will be discussed at length. A full consideration of any one of them, with all its ramifications, would require a separate study of some complexity. But, fortunately, a brief presentation will suffice to show how each provides an obstacle to holding such a position. I shall sketch out a line of possible defence against each problem raised, and shall attempt to represent the theory as sympathetically as possible. But it is my judgement that some of the problems to be indicated do constitute sufficient reason to eschew this theory and any of its counter-parts, hold to a basically traditional version of Leibniz's Law, as developed in chapter six, and either reject the metaphysical 'cross-category' identity statements which violate it, or else understand them as something other than genuinely cross-category statements of literal, numerical identity. This latter possibility will be considered briefly at the end of this chapter and also in chapter nine.

Problems for the theory

There are basically five components to the theory of regulative identity: (1) the notion of a mode of discourse, (2) an account of human language as encompassing multiple modes of discourse, (3) an understanding of the function of informative identity statements, (4) the identification of a type of identity statement which can bridge two different modes of discourse, and (5) a revision of Leibniz's Law which will allow the truth, or warranted assertability, of such identity statements. Aside from component three, which can be the understanding of identity statements presented earlier in this study, each of these elements of the theory can be questioned. Difficulties can be seen to attend each. But first, a general misgiving we might have about any such theory should be aired.

We might take note of the fact that the theory, or any of its counterparts in the philosophical literature, seems to crop up only under fairly suspicious circumstances: Some philosopher presents us with a statement (or class of statements) concerning which he claims that (i) it is an identity statement, and (ii) it is true; although he also admits that, as traditionally understood, (iii) it violates the principle giverning identity, Leibniz's Law. Does (iii) cause him to withdraw claim (i) or (ii)? No; instead, the principle, otherwise completely acceptable (let's pretend), is tinkered with. Surely, this is pretty suspect. It thus might seem that the theory of regulative identity (or any of its counter-parts) is just concocted for the quite limited purpose of saving those odd identity statements (phenomenalist, materialist, micro-theoretical, christological) to which it grants special status. But as I have presented it in the last chapter, the emendation of Leibniz's Law is rooted in some quite general considerations about human thought and language. As long as it is presented in this way, the theory of regulative identity is thus at least not obviously a mere case of special pleading. And of course, to impugn the motives of those who propose such a theory is not to impugn the theory itself. So let us look at the theory itself critically.

A much more serious kind of criticism can be made, and in fact has been made in a doctoral dissertation by Don Garrett.[1] Leaving aside the motives of those who make such an emendation of Leibniz's Law, and the question of the general justification of the theory in which it is embedded, it can be argued that it just does not work. For any apparent violation of Leibniz's Law that the theory allows some cross-mode identity statement to avoid, there is a real violation, logically related, which it cannot eliminate.

Adapted to my terminology, the kind of argument propounded by Garrett can be recounted quite easily. Consider the following statement, which might be characteristic of a physicalist metaphysic, based on an advanced neuro-science:

(N)   Mental event m is identical with neural event n,

where the mental event is an occurrent thought or sensation, and the neural event is whatever an advanced neuro-science would identify that mental event with. Treated as an identity statement, (N) can appear to violate Leibniz's Law in its traditional form. Take, for example, a predicate W, 'is located in brain region R'. Suppose that '$W(n)$' yields a true statement. The well known problem is that it seems '$W(m)$' would *not* yield a true statement. If not, then the two purportedly co-referential expressions 'm' and 'n' are such that a predicate of the right sort (actually associated with one term and in proper logical form) which joins to the one to form a true statement does not so join to the other. Something true of n is not true of m. Leibniz's Law in its classic form (L in chapter six) is thus violated by (N). On that basis, (N) would be judged false as an identity, and since the violation is conceptual, necessarily false if even meaningful at all—such that it could not even possibly be true.[2]

The emended version of Leibniz's Law ensconced in the theory of regulative identity, however, is violated *not* when there is a predicate true of one item but not true of the other, but only when there is a predicate true of one and (non-conceptually) false of the other. When the predication misfires in the case of one of two allegedly co-referential expressions, yielding a meaningless or conceptually proscribed, rather than a merely false, result, the law is not violated. Thus, on the emended version, the truth of (N) would be allowed.

However, at this point Garrett would have us consider such a predicate as 'is such as to bear meaningful attributions of intra-cranial location'. This predicate attaches to 'n' to yield a true statement. But attached to 'm' it seems clearly to yield a perfectly well formed *false* one. Thus Leibniz's Law even in its customarily emended form is violated. And the problem here is an entirely general one. For every predicate P, there is constructable a second predicate of the form 'is such as to bear meaningful attributions of _____', where the blank is filled either by the appropriate value of the phrase form ⌜the predicate P⌝ or by some determinable predicate of which P is a determinate. That is, the blank could be filled in our example either by 'the predicate "is located in R"', or by 'intra-cranial location'. Because of the generality of this possibility, no cross-mode identity statement between terms which do not share all predicates in common can escape the net of Leibniz's Law. They will be prohibited, one and all. Thus the theory of regulative identity fails to do what it was proposed to do.

This is a powerful objection to the theory; but an answer may be available. In order to perceive more clearly the structure of a possible answer, let us employ the following symbolism. Let 'W' stand for the (more general) property 'has a determinate location'. Further, let 'T' stand for the truth-value 'true', 'F' for 'contingently false', and 'M' for the assessment 'meaningless or logically false', to be applied to a declarative sentence of statement-making form which is neither true nor contingently false. The proponent of the regulative theory of identity holds that any detractor of (N) who thinks it violates Leibniz's Law because of W is probably making one or both of two mistakes. First, he may be understanding the predication of W to be assessible in the following way:

$$W(n) - T$$
$$W(m) - F$$

And secondly, he may be employing a version of Leibniz's Law such as L in chapter six which requires that both assessments be 'T'.

First of all, the regulative identity theorist proffers the version of Leibniz's Law which does not require that the two assessments be 'T' and 'T'; only that they not be 'T' and 'F' (L'), or that they not be 'empirically T' and 'empirically F' (L"). And secondly, he claims that the proper assessments of the predication of W are:

$$W(n) - T$$
$$W(m) - M$$

And this does not constitute a violation of the emended Leibniz's Law.

Now let us employ 'CW' to designate the constructable predicate 'belongs to the category of things which are such as can bear meaningful attributions of the predicate "W"'. According to the Garrett argument, the predication of CW to m and n *will* yield the following results:

$$CW(n) - T$$
$$CW(m) - F$$

And thus Leibniz's Law, even in its emended form, is violated.

But consider more carefully these two predications. They each can be understood as presenting the allocation of an individual to a category. As such, their truth values are had necessarily (of conceptual necessity).[3] It is not just contingently or empirically true that neural event n has the property CW. Nothing could be that event and lack that property. And, on the view we are considering, it is not contingently or empirically false that mental event m has it. It is necessarily, conceptually false. That is to say, there is no possible world in which something has all the essential properties of being m, or any mental event and has the property CW. On one version of the emended Leibniz's Law (L"), the assessments 'necessarily T' and 'necessarily F' do not signal or constitute a violation of it. If it is acceptable, (N) survives at this level as well as relative to the predicate W.

Thus, the theory again succeeds in saving (N) (or any like cross-mode identity) from falsehood.

But we may wonder whether there is at least some level at which the theory fails. For, surely, given a predicate such as CW, a further predicate is constructable. Call it 'CCW', the property of belonging to the category of things which belong to the category of things which can bear meaningful attributions of the predicate 'W'. However, it should be clear that at any level of such ascending predicate construction, the same solution of the problem is available. In this way, the Garrett objection can be answered. Whether the answer is very plausible is open to doubt. It is certainly arguable, and at least can look defensible, especially from the general perspective on language in which the theory is rooted. The point to be made here is that if the theory is to be appraised as successful and held, the difficulty raised by Garrett would have to be overcome in some such way.

The Garrett objection is directed against the component of the theory of regulative identity in which Leibniz's Law is emended in order to allow for the truth of cross-mode identity statements. It amounts to saying: Even if components (1)–(4) of the theory are acceptable, the whole purpose of the entire apparatus, captured in component (5), it fails to achieve. Even supposing that this overall criticism could be turned back in something like the way indicated, we still have the specifics of the theory to examine. Let us then look at its first component.

Without going into any detail here, for the relevant related literature on logical types and categories is, as I have indicated earlier, quite extensive and beyond the scope of this study to review, it should be pointed out that the notion of a mode of discourse is somewhat vague and indeterminate. How many modes of discourse are operative in the English language? An answer to this question surely would be difficult to attain, to say the least. In presenting the notion of a mode of discourse, I have mentioned some quite general criteria, following Waismann, for delimiting such a range of language, and I have suggested some paradigmatic examples which seem to satisfy the criteria and thus constitute logically different ways of carving up the world of experience. More than this, however, might be difficult to achieve.

But it is at least arguable that nothing any less vague or any more determinate is needed by the proponent of those deviant metaphysical identities we are considering. It may be clear enough that there are logical and conceptual differences between sense data talk, physical object language, micro-theoretical accounts, mentalistic discourse, and God talk, for instance. And this would be sufficient for pointing out that identity statements whose referring expressions derive from two of these ranges of language might need to be treated in some special way. Nor is it required of the metaphysician that he be able to give a complete inventory of the modes of discourse operative in any natural language. It is enough that he identify whatever two modes he wishes to link with cross-mode identities. So, arguably, the theory does not necessarily fail from any indeterminacy of the notion of a mode of discourse. But vagueness is rarely a strength. So if we accept the notion, we must do so with caution and circumspection.

Let us move on to the second component of the theory, the claim that human language encompasses multiple modes of discourse, ranges of language logically distinct. Of course, there can be no cross-mode or regulative identity statements unless there are discrete modes for them to bridge. What we need to ask at this point is whether in fact there are several logically bounded, discrete, and independent linguistic territories of the appropriate kind within any natural language.

Let us turn now to look for a moment at our theological example. If the theologian who propounds the identity of the man Jesus with a divine being is to appropriate the theory of regulative identity in order to pass his identity claim through the net of Leibniz's Law, he needs to claim the existence of two discrete modes of discourse, the human and the divine, let us say. The crucial question then is whether this latter claim can be defended. There is an interesting argument that it cannot.

Central to and partially constitutive of any mode of discourse relevant to the theory are its predicates.[4] A brief consideration of these linguistic constituents of the allegedly distinct divine mode will suffice to indicate that it will be very difficult to provide an account of it such that it can be seen to be *both* logically independent of other modes *and* intelligible. Let us first consider the alleged divine predicates.

According to the account of modes of discourse in chapter seven, these ranges of language are such that standard logical relations do not hold between them in any straightforward way. For example, no statement or conjunction of statements in one mode will entail a statement or conjunction of statements in another mode. This was the reason given for the failure of classic phenomenalism and logical behaviourism. The problem with the divine predicates is this: in so far as they are intelligible, the statements they are used to make clearly seem to entail statements in what would have to be other modes of discourse. Take for example the predicate 'omnipotent'. If God the Son is omnipotent, then he can do anything (or at least anything he wants to do—let's pretend here that no further qualifications are needed).[5] If he wants to found a religion, he can. And if Jesus *is* God the Son, then if *he* wants to found a religion, he can. Notice, it is not claimed that the identity licenses attribution to Jesus of the purportedly divine predicate of 'omnipotence'. According to the theory of regulative identity, such an attribution very well may result in meaninglessness. But it does license attributing to Jesus any predicate had by God the Son which is meaningfully ascribable to both. And if omnipotence implies the ability of an agent to do anything coherently describable which he wants to do, clearly a predicate falling within the human mode of discourse, then statements in the alleged divine mode about a divine being will entail statements in the human mode, in so far as that divine being is identical with some human individual.

The same point could be made with the predicate 'omnipresent'. If it means something like 'actively present at each and every point in space', then an individual's omnipresence will involve (its statement will entail a statement of) his active presence in South Bend, Indiana. If God is omnipresent, and God the Son is God, then it follows that God the Son is omnipresent. It thus follows that he is present in South Bend. Now, from the identity of Jesus and God the Son, it need not follow that Jesus is omnipresent. In fact it may fail to be meaningfully ascribable to him. But certainly presence in South Bend is at least meaningfully ascribable to any man. It is a predication within the scope of the human mode of discourse. So from the identity, it *will* follow that Jesus is actively present in South Bend.

And surely such entailments are unacceptable to the theory. They may appear unacceptable in two ways. First, it may seem that they will result in violations of Leibniz's Law for the christological indentities. But that is not the problem in focus here. The point here is that the entailments cross what are supposed to be logically discrete modes of discourse. In order to preserve the divine mode as distinct in the appropriate way, it would seem that we will have to understand the divine predicates in some other way. An account of them must be given which does not involve entailments into what would have to be another mode of discourse.

But how else are we to spell out the meaning of the divine predicates? It is not at all clear. In so far as they are intelligible, they do not seem to be logically independent of the human mode of discourse. And in so far as they are held to be independent, they would seem not to be intelligible. Even firm proponents of the doctrine of analogical predication would accept such modest entailments as those just mentioned, else they would find themselves among the blatantly heterodox. For if 'omnipotent' and 'omnipresent' do not have such meanings as are assumed above, what *do* they mean?

We seem to have raised here a serious problem. And I think strictly analogous arguments could be applied to the claim that there is a discrete mode of sense-data discourse, or a logically independent range of mentalistic discourse. It is well known, for example, that sense-data descriptions are unable to avoid physical object terms. Phenomenalists have spoken of, say, table-like sensa. And so forth. On the basis of such arguments it can seem that we must reject the second component of the theory of regulative identity. And if this goes, the theory as a whole goes.

But, once again, it not entirely obvious that this problem is beyond solution. It could be suggested that it is not necessary for the notion of a mode of discourse that such a conceptual system be *totally* isolated logically from other such systems. The only thing needed to make the theory of regulative identity work is the claim that *not all* logical relations hold between modes. It need not be claimed that no such relations hold. Modes of discourse need not be completely disjoint in order to be appropriately distinct and discrete.

Given this distinction, the points made above about the divine predicates need not be taken to rule out there being a distinguishable divine mode of discourse. And, likewise, analogous arguments concerning logical and conceptual relations and dependencies between other alleged modes need not be taken to rule out their integrity as such ranges of language as are required by the theory. By such a response, the second component of the theory might at this point pass scrutiny.

However, there is another problem which can be raised for these first two components of the theory. It can be posed in more than one way. First of all, the understanding of language as encompassing all these different ways of carving up our experience of the world seems to involve a severe anti-realism concerning properties.[6] We seem to be precluded from talking about what properties objects really have and restricted to talk about subjects and predicates within a mode of discourse only. Or we can put the problem in another way, making reference to the distinction drawn between logical and ontological subjects in the presentation of the theory in chapter seven.

In the theory, ontological subjects underly logical subjects as constituting the fundamental 'furniture of the universe'. An actually referring expression within a mode of discourse has as its available referent a logical subject, identifiable and describable only within that mode. But a logical subject is the form or guise of some ontological subject accessible to that mode. The same ontological subject may be accessible in two different modes in the form of two different logical subjects. It is this which allows for cross-mode or regulative identity statements joining two very different logical subjects.

The problem is this. Every ordinary, straight-forward statement presumably is made within a mode of discourse. Everything we say is *ex hypothesi* about logical subjects. The ontological subjects which lie, necessarily, *behind* all our talk thus appear to be the most remote of substrata or substances 'we know not what'. And, to quote Austin Farrer:[7]

But 'we know not what' is what we do not know, and it is difficult to put so nondescript an article on the philosophical market.

It is important for the theory of regulative identity that behind its alleged multiple modes of discourse lie such 'bare' particulars. And the lack of attractiveness of any such position is, of course, notorious.

So the charge is that the theory is committed to a severe anti-realist position with regard to properties and correspondingly to a fundamental ontology of the barest of particulars. Surely this lessens the attractiveness of the theory, to say the least. Of course, as always, there is a possible rebuttal. The charge assumes that for the theory all modes of discourse are more or less equal, in the sense of being equally removed from the items which fundamentally exist in the world. It is open to a proponent of the theory to claim some particular mode to be 'privileged', to give somehow direct access to ontological subjects.[8] This move would be most plausible, possibly, with physical object discourse. One could then be 'realist' with respect to properties expressed in the favoured mode, and thereby have some garb for the otherwise bare particulars. In this way the charge could be neutralised. But it might be a difficult position to develop and defend.

There is only one remaining internal problem for the theory which I want to sketch out. It is, I believe, the most difficult to solve. I call it 'the countability problem'. It stands as an obstacle to component (4) of the theory, the claim that there can be identity statements bridging two different modes of discourse.

Whereas we may have thought that the two referring expressions in an informative identity statement referred to two different objects, the import of such a statement is to present them as referring only to one. In order to ascertain its truth, we thus need to be able to count the number of objects referred to. It would seem that among the necessary conditions for the truth of an identity statement is the condition that the referents of its referring expressions be countable. In fact, we might specify more carefully that no sentence can be used to make an identity statement unless it contains two referring expressions, and no linguistic item can be a referring expression unless it is used in association with a general concept which carries with it principles for individuation, counting, and re-identification of objects. Now 'object', like 'thing', 'entity', 'individual', 'particular', and 'referent', is a count noun. But, also like them, it is not a sortal term. It does not have associated with its use the requisite principles. It has, rather, been dubbed a 'dummy sortal'. Its occurrence in a sentence holds a place for a sortal term. Thus, only those uses of 'object' and the other dummy sortals are legitimate which could in principle be replaced by use of some sortal.

When we say that an identity statement presents us with two referring expressions as referring to only one *object*, we have to remember that in the case of any particular statement, we must in principle be able to specify further, 'namely, one_____', where the blank is filled by some sortal term. And, of course, in order to make this specification, there must be at least some one sortal under which both the two referring expressions of the identity statement have their uses. Otherwise, we can judge neither that they have two referents nor that they share one in common. And this is a logical, rather than a physical, impossibility.

It will be clear that this claim resembles in one respect the position espoused by Peter Geach, that the sentence frame for identity, '_____ is _____' is incomplete, needing attachment of a sortal term to the identity sign for its logical completion.[9] But I see no reason to hold such sentences to be incomplete. I prefer the term 'expandable'. Every standard use of a referring expression depends on some associated sortal, contextually understood if not explicitly invoked. So, the filling of the blanks which will result in the making of an identity statement involves already the employment of at least one sortal. Thus, in so far as the above sentence frame is used to make an identity statement, there is no real incompleteness for the removal of which augmentation of the identity sign is needed. My thesis I call 'the expandability thesis'. It is akin to Wiggin's thesis of Sortal Dependency. I believe that it should be uncontroversial.

But whether we talk of the identity frame '_____ is _____' being incomplete in Geach's sense, or expandable in mine, a serious problem arises for the very possibility of regulative identity statements. For if the two referring expressions derive from logically different modes of discourse, it would seem to be doubtful that they are governed by any one sortal in common. And this is a necessary condition for their having one referent in common. Their referents cannot be counted together as one or two or anything unless there is at least one sortal under which they both function. If this condition is not met, we have not a false identity, but no identity statement at all. Intelligibility as an identity statement requires countability, and countability precludes logical independence between the two referring expressions. If the object(s) presented are not countable, no identity can be asserted.

The various modes of discourse operative in human language have been presented as logically and conceptually distinct ranges of language. We would be hard put to find any one sortal in each of two different modes. What kind of object is both a kind of sensum *and* a kind of material object, or a kind of material object *and* a kind of mental entity? An answer to these questions would appear to be hard to find, if possible at all. If modes of discourse are logically distinct as the theory of regulative identity suggests, then we would not expect to find one and the same sortal embedded in two different modes. But if no such sortal can be found, no identity statement can bridge two modes. There can thus be no regulative identities.

A defender of regulative identity might concede that without a sortal common to the two expressions flanking the verb 'to be' in a regulative identity statement it cannot be claimed that the number of their referent(s) is one. But he might suggest that all the regulative statement need be taken as doing is presenting in effect the *denial* that they are two. This might be thought to effect the kind of ontological reduction or simplifying for which the regulative identity statement is employed.

But this will not work. The denial that two linguistic expressions have two referents will be true under any one of three different conditions: (1) they both refer, but are co-referential, (2) only one of them has a referent (the other being either a non-referential expression, or a referential expression which fails of reference), (3) neither of them has a referent (for either of the above reasons). It is only the first condition which any identity statement presents as holding.

This is the only kind of move available once it is agreed that the two expressions flanking the verb 'to be' in an alleged regulative identity statement share no one sortal in common. And it does not work. But, again, the question which must be asked is whether the notion of a mode of discourse requires that they be so logically separate as to have no sortals in common. As I already have suggested, the mere claim that different modes are logically distinct need not be taken to imply total separation between them. It thus may seem possible that referring expressions from two different modes of discourse logically distinguishable have their use under some sortal common to both modes. It may be embedded in both modes, or may have its fundamental use in one, a derivative use in the other. A further pursuit of this line of reasoning, of this construal of the notion of a mode of discourse, would, if acceptable, show countability not to be a problem. It would eliminate this difficulty for the theory of regulative identity. But I am seriously doubtful that this can be done.

I know of no proof that it cannot be done, that this move cannot work. But as I have suggested already, it just seems impossible to specify any *kind* of object which is, or even could be, both a collection of sensa and a physical object, or a material entity and a Cartesian mental item. I know of no genuine sortal whose associated principles are so liberal as to allow for the individuation of logically or categorially heterogeneous items, items falling within logically discrete modes of discourse. Now of course it is possible to concoct such a sortal (with a disjunctive set of associated principles), but I do not think that the serious metaphysician who might want to employ the theory of regulative identity would be satisfied with such an artificial contrivance. Thus there seems to be no *plausible* way out of the countability problem.

At least five serious problems have been raised for the theory of regulative identity. I have tried to be as sympathetic to the theory as possible and sketch out the direction a solution to each problem would have to take. But at least some of the lines of defence are less than fully plausible. On closer scrutiny, I believe they would be found clearly unacceptable. It is my opinion that these difficulties conspire to render the theory unacceptable. No conclusive proof has been presented to show that the theory fails. But such positions rarely fall to conclusive disproof. I have chosen rather to make clear what we might call the 'logical price' of holding such a position—the burden of resolving such problems as those presented—a price I myself consider prohibitive. Thus if I am right, there is no defensible theoretical justification along these lines for emending Leibniz's Law to allow the truth of deviant, cross-category metaphysical identity statements. If these statements must all be taken as literal statements of the numerical identity of categorially heterogeneous individuals, we must judge them to be false, one and all. But I am not convinced that they should all be so taken. In the next section, I shall explore the possibility that some identity statements which appear to violate Leibniz's Law are to be understood as metaphorical in nature. In his recent book *Sorts, Ontology, and Metaphor*, Shalom Lappin has contended that all cross-category (or in his terms, 'sortally incorrect') predications should be understood metaphorically.[10] It might be tempting to adopt the same view concerning all apparently cross-category identities. I hope to show the value and limitations of applying this perspective to the identity statements we have been considering.

Metaphorical identities

In this short section, I want to sketch out briefly another way in which it might be claimed that deviant identity statements are to be understood. It is well known that standard statement forms admit of instances which if taken literally yield something false or nonsensical, but if understood in some non-standard way communicate important insight. Articulating insight in this way has long been thought to be the exclusive province of poets. But just recently, philosophers increasingly have come to recognise the general importance of metaphor and other non-literal usage in human language and thought. It might be suggested that deviant cross-category identities, which if taken to be literal statements of numerical identity must be assessed as false, should be understood rather as metaphorical identities.

In this way they still could be claimed to express, in some suitably extended sense, truth.

Anthropologists are fairly accustomed to coming across the serious enunciation of rather bizarre statements of identity. A typical sort of case might go something like this: At about the time of the winter solstice when a particular tribe begins to worry that the sun may take its leave from them permanently, they build a fire in the centre of the village and proclaim 'This fire is the sun'. They then care for the fire and keep it going, thereby, or rather there*in*, keeping the sun alive. It is as obvious to them as it is to us that the village fire and the sun are not literally, numerically identical. Is their statement then a statement of what has been called 'qualitative identity'? Not obviously. Doing something to an object merely *like* the sun, in however many respects, is not doing something to the sun. So this might be said to be a case of metaphorical identity.

Consider a more familiar case. In the Christian Eucharist, the presentation of bread is accompanied by a repetition of Jesus' proclamation 'This is my body', and the wine by his statement 'This is my blood'. These cannot be statements of literal, numerical identity and be true. And it might be argued that not even a scrupulous protestant would hold them to be only assertations of qualitative identity, to the effect that the bread and wine merely resemble the body and blood of Christ to some extent. So it might be concluded that they are metaphorical identities.

One final case. Suppose you are dealing with a person whom you take to be a field representative of Philosophical Publishing, Incorporated. Unknown to you, he is the Chairman of the Board, President, and active Editor-in-Chief. You wonder aloud what Philosophical Publishing would think of something he has said to you, and he replies 'I *am* Philosophical Publishing'. Certainly, this again is neither a literal numerical identity, nor a statement of qualitative identity. He is not saying that he is *like* the company in all, or any, respects. Thus, it might be suggested that this also is a case of metaphorical identity.

From examples such as these, it might be thought that we need to recognise a kind of identity statement not usually acknowledged in the literature on identity, a metaphorical or non-literal variety. If this is so, then we can entertain the suggestion that some cross-category identities are statements of a non-literal sort. As metaphorical identities, it might be said, we should take them seriously but not literally. The problems seen to attend the understanding of them as literal statements of numerical identity might then be dismissed as irrelevant to an appreciation of them as metaphorically conveying great insight of some kind.

According to such a position, metaphorical identity statements would be syntactically isomorphic with their literal counter-parts. Semantically, both kinds of statement would be made by means of two referring expressions flanking the verb 'to be' whose order of occurrence as subject or predicate nominative would not affect the statement made. And pragmatically (to employ the third member of this well known triad of linguistic categories), both would be connected with the merging of bodies of information, and the consequent warranting of certain beliefs and expectations, along with the licensing of certain forms of intentional behaviour, otherwise inappropriate. But the pragmatics would diverge to the extent that merging or collating of bodies of information in the case of metaphorical identities would not be complete, unlike the case of literal numerical identities. The former, unlike the latter, would not strictly obey Leibniz's Law. It would govern them only with a loose hand, so to speak.

This pragmatic divergence would be rooted in a fundamental semantic difference. The two referring expressions in a metaphorical identity statement would not be literally co-referential. That is to say, within a limited context, and for limited, contextually relative purposes they would be *treated as* co-referential; but they would not in fact *be* co-referential. This is the crucial difference.

Needless to say, most metaphysicians and theologians would not be very happy at having any of their central doctrines classified together with magic and hyperbole. Nevertheless, some might prefer having their pronouncements accepted as metaphor over having them rejected as falsehood. I think it unfortunate that a surprisingly sizeable faction of *avant garde* theologians actually do take this way out in christology. The question is whether such a position is acceptable. Two *caveats* should be issued from the start. First of all, the examples presented to illustrate the kind of case which might be labelled as a metaphorical identity should not for a moment mislead us into thinking of metaphorical identity statements as somehow stronger than qualitative identities yet weaker than their literal analogues, and as intermediate in that sense. And secondly, we should scrutinise all such alleged cases to see whether the verb 'to be' is not more accurately understood as functioning in one of its capacities other than that of an identity expression.

These precautions heeded, the real problem attending such a position would seem to be very simple. We and the natives know the fire is not *really* identical with the sun. The President of Philosophical Publishing does not pretend to be really the same entity as his company. But proponents of metaphysically important cross-category identity statements for the most part do not share this frame of mind. They are not usually content to have their claims taken seriously but not literally. It seems that any position which countenances their pronouncements only at the expense of removing them from the realm of the literal will thus fail to be serviceable in the way needed.

In light of the problems attending the theory of regulative identity, I think it is most reasonable to conclude that if an identity statement is genuinely cross-category, it must be understood as metaphorical in order to be accepted as true. Thus, in any case where a metaphorical treatment is unacceptable and yet the identity in question is to be affirmed, the only option remaining is to deny that it is genuinely cross-category in semantic or conceptual status, in spite of any appearances to the contrary. In recent years, some philosophers have explored this sort of strategy to explicate and defend a favoured form of apparently cross-category identity. An interesting set of papers, for example, by Stuart Rosenbaum and James Cornman which appeared a few years ago briefly explore this way of understanding micro-theoretical and mental-neural identities.[11] In the next chapter, I would like to focus on that apparently cross-category identity not discussed by many contemporary philosophers, the foundational identity of Christian theology, and see how this strategy might work in its case, since it may appear to be the most extremely deviant of all the unusual identity statements we have considered.

9

A Case Study

Identity and incarnation

In recent years, there has been increasing interest in the philosophy of religion, and in particular in Christian philosophical theology. Quite a bit of energy and ingenuity has been expended in trying to articulate as clearly as possible and evaluate beliefs fundamental to the Christian faith. And surely this has paid some important philosophical dividends. Consider, for example, how any careful scrutiny of the ontological argument is bound to crystallise and focus a number of basic and difficult issues in philosophical logic and metaphysics. But, understandably, philosophers have tended to concentrate their attention on the general elements of theism which underlie Christian belief rather than on uniquely Christian affirmations. Consequently, some striking claims with significant metaphysical implications have been relatively ignored in the recently growing literature. Central among those relatively neglected claims is the doctrine of the Incarnation, on which most distinctively Christian theology is built. The core of this doctrine is the claim that the man Jesus of Nazareth was himself God, or more specifically God the Son, the Second Person of the divine Trinity, everlasting creator of heaven and earth. Anyone with even a little knowledge of classical theism will recognise immediately that this is quite an extraordinary identity claim. It has been widely thought an absurd claim, even by some within the church. Tertullian and Kierkegaard, for example, seemed to value it especially on this account. But many contemporary theologians have been somewhat less willing to embrace what appears to them to be obvious paradox. A surprising number of them even go out of their way to denounce the christological identity as, variously, unintelligible, incoherent, and literally meaningless.

Of all the odd identity claims we have been considering, the incarnational claim indeed can seem the oddest. The God of theism and any human being can appear to be as far apart categorially or conceptually as any alleged entities might possibly be. And the christological claim obviously lacks the kind of general theoretical motivation and backing other apparently cross-category identities can boast. It is no wonder then that it has evoked a great deal of intellectual perplexity whenever it has been thought about philosophically.

On the basis of what was argued in the last chapter, I think we can reasonably say that if the christological identity were genuinely a cross-category statement, as it admittedly appears to be, contemporary theologians would be right in rejecting it, or treating it as at best mere metaphor. But I want to suggest that despite surface appearances, even this most extraordinary of identities need not be taken as genuinely cross-categorial. In fact, I think it is only some serious, but understandable intellectual mistakes which result in its having to be treated as a cross-category claim. Once we get clear on the sort of concept of God and of man properly ingredient in Christian theology, we shall see that the christological identity can be understood as a constitutive one, conceptually non-deviant, and thus a legitimate candidate for the satisfaction of Leibniz's Law, as traditionally construed. If this strategy is plausible in the christological case, it surely may be in other cases of apparently cross-category identity as well. The only plausible defence of any apparently deviant identity of metaphysical import as a literal statement of numerical identity lies in showing that deviance to be a surface phenomenon alone, due to an inappropriate perspective, or set of philosophical assumptions brought to an assessment of it.

Let us examine the christological identity:

(C)   Jesus is God the Son.

'Jesus' is of course here intended to designate a man known to have lived in first-century Palestine. He is believed to have been born of Jewish parentage, to have lived for at least a short time as an itinerant preacher, and to have died by crucifixion. 'God the Son' is intended to designate a divine being, a supernatural person with all the attributes essential to deity. Christians often express the doctrine of the Incarnation by saying that in the person of Jesus, God became a man. So (C) presents us with a case of identity in which one individual is supposed to have all the essential properties of being human as well as of being God. The Christ was, according to orthodoxy, 'fully God and fully man'.

The problems for such a claim have been obvious since it was first propounded. Theistic philosophers and theologians have always emphasised the great difference between divine and human properties, and never have failed to realise the difficulty this creates for the doctrine of the Incarnation. God is, for example, traditionally supposed to be omnipotent, omniscient, and omnipresent. Every man is limited with respect to power, knowledge, and presence. Humans are the sort of beings who, whether or not they can ever cease to exist, can and do begin to exist. But God is everlasting. Furthermore, we are all contingent beings. God is a necessary being. So in the case of humanity and divinity, we seem to have not only divergent, but logically disparate and metaphysically incompatible sets of properties not jointly satisfiable by any one being. It thus appears that Leibniz's Law is violated by (C) many times over in the most metaphysically extreme sort of way.

Accordingly, theologian Don Cupitt draws the conclusion that:[1]

> The eternal God, and a historical man, are two beings of quite different ontological status. It is simply unintelligible to declare them identical.

And John Hick, in his inimitable way, says:[2]

> 'Jesus is God' is as devoid of meaning as 'This circle is a square'.

Theologians who reject (C) rarely are content to call it false. Their argument (when they are at all explicit about giving one) is that it violates Leibniz's Law. But when an identity statement violates Leibniz's Law, it is judged false. Yet detractors of incarnation almost always categorise (C) in the ways represented by Hick and Cupitt, as unintelligible, incoherent, or meaningless. Aside from any possible desires just to be as rhetorically iconoclastic as possible, I think these critics use these particular terms of disapprobation because they view (C) as being false not only necessarily, but also *a priori*. They see it as semantically deviant or conceptually skewed. They understand it, in short, as a cross-category identity. The assumption is that the concept of God and the concept of a human person logically are not co-exemplifiable by one and the same individual.

Resisting this sort of rejection of (C), the Reverend Brian Hebblethwaite has protested:[3]

> But 'God' and 'man' are far from being such tightly defined concepts. It is difficult enough to suppose that we have a full and adequate grasp of what it is to be a human being. We certainly have no such grasp of the divine nature. Who are we to say that the essence of God is such as to rule out the possibility of his making himself present in the created world as a human being, while in no way ceasing to be the God he ever is?

Hebblethwaite's point is simple: We are not in a proper epistemic position to justifiably categorize the christological identity as necessarily and *a priori* false. We are not in a position to know its conceptual status to be that of a cross-category statement. In this respect, among others, it is quite different from any claim that some circle is a square. Presumably, Hebblethwaite would agree that if (C) were cross-categorial, it could not serve as the literal statement of numerical identity the church has taken it to be. That is why he would resist this understanding of it.

I think Hebblethwaite is on to something important. Jesus was non-identical with God the Son only if there is some property Jesus had, but God the Son lacks, or vice versa. The identity is absurd, and so forth, only if the one had properties not possibly exemplified by, or not even meaning-fully ascribable to, the other. The question which must be asked is: How do we know of such a divergence in properties or meaningful predications?

Conceptual construction

In an article entitled 'God's Death', A D Smith presented a few years ago the only extended argument in recent literature against the coherence of the incarnational claim. At one point in the argument, he stated:[4]

> If Christ is God, then he cannot have begun to exist at a certain point in human history because God (and his Son) are necessarily eternal. But then nothing can count as a man, a creature, which does not have a beginning in time and which is thus coeval with God.

The remark about 'counting as a man' makes clear the sort of reasoning engaged in by Smith, Hick, and Cupitt, among other critics of incarnation. Smith is relying on a certain sort of conception of human nature and divine nature for the generation of his argument.

According to one standard account of natural kinds, every such kind has an essence, a set of properties or underlying traits individually necessary and jointly sufficient for membership in the kind. We can understand divine nature and human nature, or divinity and humanity, in a parallel fashion. Human nature comprises all those properties individually necessary and jointly sufficient for being human. No individual can be human without having each and every one of the properties essential to humanity. And likewise for divinity. On the traditional doctrine of God, properties essential for divinity include omnipotence, omniscience, aseity, eternality and the like. Essential human properties are, interestingly, not so easy to list.

Specifications of what properties are essential to particular kinds constitute what Stephen Schwartz has called 'stable generalizations'— propositions which are necessarily true (with 'broadly logical' necessity), but known only *a posteriori*.[5] Perhaps the most reasonable way of understanding kind-essences will yield the result that no non-trivial kind-essential properties are known to characterise particular kinds *a priori*. In this respect, divinity and humanity would then seem to differ from natural kinds. The epistemic status of many, if not all, of the known attributes essential to deity can be argued to be known to be such *a priori*. And it may be that at least one non-trivial essential human property is so known—the modal property of possibly being conscious at some time. But most non-trivial essential human properties will not be known *a priori*. They will, like properties non-trivially essential to any natural kind, be known only *a posteriori*. In this respect, the concept of humanity differs from merely constructed concepts such as that of a square, a circle, a home-run, or, in a slightly different way, that of a bachelor.

If such properties as those of possibly being annihilated, having a beginning in time, and metaphysical contingency were essential human properties, any truly human being would have to exemplify each of them. Thus Jesus, if he was fully human, would have had them, and the incarnational identity would be conceptually ruled out. For surely these are properties no divine person could possibly have. In an attempt to deal with the problem Leibniz's Law creates for the incarnational claim, a number of nineteenth century theologians employed a clever strategy whose result came to be known generically as 'kenotic christology'. God, remember, is unlimited in power, knowledge, and presence. Any man is limited in these respects. The kenoticists thought they could circumvent the difficulties therein arising for incarnation by claiming that God the Son temporarily 'laid down', or limited his exercise of, his otherwise unlimited attributes during the sojourn of the incarnation. However, the properties I have just mentioned concerning the metaphysical status of an object's existence clearly do not admit this manoeuvre. An everlasting being cannot lay aside his eternity and begin to exist. A necessary being cannot become contingent. These are logical impossibilities available not even to a God with the most extraordinary powers of self-limitation. So if we could know such properties as contingency to be essential human properties, we could know (C) to be cross-category and so not possibly true in any literal sense. But the question we must press here is: What reason do we have to believe that such properties are essential human properties, necessary elements of what it is to be human?

In order to be able to appreciate the impact of this question, we first must take care to draw a clear, but among theologians rarely acknowledged, distinction between *common* human properties and *essential* ones. A common human property will be one which many or most human beings have. A limiting case of commonality would be a property which was shared by all humans alike. We need to be clear that a property's being common or even universal for members of a kind does not entail that it is essential for the kind, such that membership in the kind would be impossible apart from its exemplification.

For example, the property of living at some time on the surface of the earth is a common human property. I think it is safe to assume that it is now a universal property for humans. But it is not an element of human nature. It is not essential for being human. It is clearly possible that at some time in the future, human beings be born, live, and die on a space station or on another planet colonised by earth, without ever setting foot on the earth itself. This is an obvious example of our distinction. The property of living at some time on the surface of the earth may now be a universal human property, but it is not an essential one.

As I have mentioned, this important distinction is often overlooked by theologians. Richard Norris, for example, has written:[6]

> We can speak of human nature, meaning something like 'that which is normally characteristic of human beings'.

I would not want to deny that Norris' use of the phrase 'human nature' is an allowable one in colloquial or informal contexts. But it certainly is not the one which properly operates in metaphysics. We need something much more precise and demanding than that for philosophical or theological anthropology. It is normally characteristic of human beings to have hair. Yet one can certainly be fully human, exemplify human nature, while lacking this adornment. It is also normally characteristic of human beings to come into existence and to have the metaphysical status of contingency. But our contemporary theologians who reject the doctrine of the Incarnation as absurd need to block the possibility of there being a man who lacks these properties. So their position depends on the more precise and demanding essentialist understanding of human nature I have noted. They thus need to acknowledge there to be a distinction between common properties and essential ones.

But once we do acknowledge a clear distinction between commonality and essence, what forces the Christian to count as essential any common human properties which would preclude a literal divine incarnation? I can think of nothing which would do this. If Christians develop their philosophical anthropology and their doctrine of God in isolation from each other and from the central tenets of Christian faith, it is no surprise that conceptual conflicts may arise, that 'impossibilities' be generated. But it is a perfectly proper procedure (some would even say—rightly I think— mandatory) for the Christian philosopher or theologian to develop his idea of human nature, his conception of what the essential human properties are, with certain presuppositions or controls derived from his doctrine of

God and his belief in the reality of the Incarnation. In a moment of rare insight, John MacQuarrie recently wrote:[7]

> Part of the trouble with the doctrine of incarnation is that we discuss the divinity and even the humanity of Christ in terms of ready-made ideas of God and man that we bring with us, without allowing these ideas to be corrected and even drastically changed by what we learn about God and man in and through Jesus Christ.

This is precisely the problem. It is all a matter of epistemic priorities. It is quite rational for the orthodox Christian to argue that we are less sure that human nature comprises properties incompatible with a divine incarnation than Christians are that Jesus was God incarnate. This is not to say that the doctrine of the Incarnation should or even could have complete epistemic priority for the Christian over any conception of humanity or divinity. Some idea of what it is to be God and what it is to be a man is required for even understanding the doctrine at all. But the conceptions requisite for understanding the doctrine at all are far from complete and unalterable.

Some few contemporary theologians who have written on the topic seem to have recognised that we can understand human nature in such a way that it is co-exemplifiable with divinity in one and the same subject. Herbert McCabe, for one, has said:[8]

> A human person just is a person with a human nature, and it makes absolutely no difference to the logic of this whether the same person does or does not exist from eternity as divine.

Surely, no *merely* human being will have existed from eternity as divine. A mere human will furthermore be a contingent creation. But no orthodox theologian ever has claimed that Jesus was *merely* human. The claim is that he was *fully* human, but also divine. If contingency, coming into existence, and possibly ceasing to exist were essential human properties, the doctrine of the Incarnation would involve a metaphysical, or broadly logical, impossibility, if not just arrant absurdity. The christological identity would be a cross-category statement, and thus would fail to express any proposition of numerical identity which could be in any literal sense true. But I can think of no compelling argument, or any other type of reason, to conclude that such properties are indeed elements of human nature, understood along precise essentialist lines.

It may be that such properties are essential to being *merely* human. Any being which exemplifies human nature without also exemplifying something like divine nature would then have to exemplify them, otherwise it would not 'count as' a mere human. But the traditional Christian claim is that in order to be fully human, it is not necessary to be merely human. An individual is merely human just in case it has all the properties requisite for being fully human (the component properties of human nature) *and also* some limitation properties as well, properties such as that of coming into existence at some time and existing contingently. On an orthodox Christian view, neither these nor any other properties logically or conceptually incompatible with a divine incarnation will be understood as elements of basic human nature at all, but rather as universal accompaniments of humanity in the case of any created human being.

The traditional Christian will hold it to be true that the body of Jesus came into being at a certain point in human history. And, lest he fall into Appolinarianism, he must acknowledge that Jesus' human consciousness came into being as well. But the ultimate metaphysical subject, the person who was Jesus and was also divine, did not himself come into existence. A person is not identical with his body. One need not be a Cartesian to see this. Nor is a person identical with any particular range of conscious experience which he may happen to have. Thus, the necessity of God the Son, and his everlasting continuance in existence, need not imply any absurdities for the Incarnation. It is in no way implied by the account just adumbrated that the body or human personality of Jesus eternally pre-existed his stay on earth. Nor is it implied that his human range of consciousness encompassed within itself, or even had any sort of direct epistemic access to, the fullness of omniscience. The humanity of Jesus, even with respect to the innermost thoughts of his earthly consciousness, need not be sacrificed or attenuated in the least to allow for the straightforward, literal truth of the incarnational identity claim.

A conclusion

I have just presented the most minimal sketch of the sort of strategy an orthodox Christian could deploy in favor of understanding the extraordinary christological identity claim as a non-deviant statement which does not on conceptual grounds run afoul of Leibniz's Law as traditionally formulated. A great many of the details necessary for making such a case have gone completely unmentioned. My purpose here is not to construct an argument in defense of theological orthodoxy on the question of the nature of the person of Christ. It is much more modest. I have intended my remarks only to exemplify a general point. What can appear at first to be clearly a cross-category identity can in various ways be argued not to bridge ultimately distinct, conceptually disparate modes of discourse, but rather to function semantically as an ordinary statement of numerical identity standing under the governance of Leibniz's Law. And this is, I think an important point.

I believe that this general sort of strategy is the only plausible way to defend an apparently cross-category identity as a literally true statement. Thus, if physicalist, phenomenalist, or micro-theoretical identities are to be, any of them, understood as statements of numerical identity and also accepted as literally true, or even possibly true, it must be shown that any apparently conceptual deviance attending them is in some such way eliminable. Of course, the specific moves necessary in any such case would be interestingly different from the details of the christological reasoning just sketched. A defender of physicalist identities would not, for example, make anything like the same sort of distinctions relied upon by the defender of traditional christology. One of his aims, however, would have to be the same—to show that the identified entities do not in fact differ categorially, or irreconcilably, in properties. Part of this project would be, presumably, the rejection of some central Cartesian characterisations of mental entities. The phenomenalist would have his own tactical problems in the pursuit of this general sort of strategy. And anyone inclined to reconcile any sort of common sense realism with a version of scientific realism would have his distinctive tasks in the recommendation of micro-theoretical identities as ultimately non-deviant statements about the world.

But in each case, the strictures of Leibniz's Law in its traditional form (as understood in chapter six) would have to be respected; else the defender of the apparently deviant identity would incur the serious logical price of defending the theory of regulative identity against problems which seem just too serious to admit of any solution which will be so plausible as to carry conviction. Because of those problems, I think we are justified in holding that a conceptually unrevised Leibniz's Law is the touchstone of warranted assertion, and thereby of truth, in matters of identity. It is ultimately the basis on which we assess, and thus assert and accept, identity statements. No favoured identity claims of metaphysical import, however deviant in appearance, ought to make us think otherwise. They must be so understood as to satisfy the simple, unrestricted Leibniz's Law, or as strict metaphysical identities they must be relinquished.

Notes

INTRODUCTION

1 Saul Kripke [2], p. 309.

CHAPTER 1

1 I am assuming this thumbnail sketch of astronomical history given in philosophical discussions of identity as a useful fiction. One of the simplifying pretences we allow ourselves is that the ancients spoke in English.

2 For example, John Woods [2], says: '... the identity relation does *not* obtain pairwise between elements from its field; identity's equivalence classes are singletons, never couples' (p. 70). *See also* Hector-Neri Castañeda [1], p. 122.

3 Panoyot Butchvarov [1], p. 13, says: 'If the statement "a is b" is true, then it is about the same thing the statement "a is a" (or "b is b") is about and also says about this thing what the latter statement says, namely that it is identical with what may only be itself.'

4 I do not, of course, mean to imply that such is the case for all necessary statements. But I do not believe anyone would deny that what I say here is true of necessary statements of the form of (1), which is all that is required by the argument being given. I should mention that Mark Platts [1], pp. 145–6, denies that any sentences of the form of (1) express propositions with the epistemic status of *a priori*. Platts just seems to overlook the sense of *a priori* I rely on here and which I sketch out in a bit more detail in chapter two, section three. On my view it is impossible to understand (1) and yet not know its truth value. There are logicians who would regard (1) as necessary, as well as *a priori*, in the strongest of senses, holding it to be true even in worlds in which Phosphorus does not exist. For this view, *see* Dana Scott [1], pp. 181–200, and Richard Grandy [1], pp. 137–55.

5 Alvin Plantinga [2], pp. 81–7.

6 Plantinga says of sentences that they 'express propositions'. In discussing his remarks, I shall use this locution rather than my own preferred term 'statement' to indicate what is said when an indicative sentence is uttered under the appropriate conditions.

7 Plantinga retracts this claim in [1].

8 I use 'P' and 'P1' as names here, not as variables. Plantinga's view of propositions is such that they can bear the reference of such referring expressions.

9 Kripke [2].

10 Kripke [1].

11 Kripke [2], pp. 260–4.

12 This appropriate simile is, I think, due to Ruth Barcan Marcus.

13 For Kripke's brief remarks on reflective relations, *see* his [2], p. 350, fn. 50.

14 It must be mentioned that Kripke draws a distinction between strong and weak necessity. A statement is strongly necessary if and only if it is true in every possible world in which the objects mentioned therein exist, *and* those objects exist in every possible world. It is weakly necessary if the first condition holds, but the objects exist only in some, but not all, possible worlds. He thus presents S as weakly necessary, since 'Venus exists' is not a (strongly) necessary truth.

15 Kripke is not altogether clear on all this. He wants to offer identity statements such as the one made with S as examples of necessary, *a posteriori* truths. But he maintains that a statement is *a priori* if there are circumstances in which it *can* be known *a priori*. Since we thus are forced to say of the statement made by S that it is both *a posteriori* and *a priori*, to avoid inconsistency it seems we must speak of it as having one or the other of these properties *relative* to its expression in a certain sentence. He himself does not specify this, and thus has been taken by some critics to be inconsistent at this point. See, for example, Michael Tye [1], p. 220, for a related change of inconsistency which is easily turned aside by this simple clarification. For a different interpretation, *see* Pavel Tichy [1].

16 See Kripke [1], p. 154.

17 Kripke [2], pp. 333–4.

18 Ibid. p. 303.

19 Kripke [1], pp. 138–9.

20 ibid. p. 139.

21 Cf. David Shwayder [1], p. 30.

22 See Shwayder [1], p. 30. He says: '. . . identities do not *state* the existence of objects to which reference is made.'

23 Robert Stalnaker [1].

24 Ibid. pp. 89–90.

25 Ibid.

26 Ibid. For a related argument and claim, *see* G W Fitch [1]. In a recent article Pavel Tichy [1], p. 232, labels the contingent proposition the proposition 'associated with' the strict identity and writes: 'To say of an object that it is identical with itself is to assert a tautology; as a consequence, sentences expressive of such identities are hardly ever uttered in order to convey what they express. The aim of uttering such a sentence is usually to create evidence for the proposition associated with it. This at any rate is what my own aim is when I sometimes introduce myself to strangers saying, briefly, "I am Pavel Tichy".'

27 Ludwig Wittgenstin [1], 5.5303. *See also* an echo of this in Frank Ramsey, 'The Foundations of Mathematics', in Ramsey [1], p. 16. And compare John Wisdom, 'Ostentation', in Wisdom [1], p. 5.

28 Again, I am not saying that all metaphysically necessary statements are empirically uninformative; but surely it will be admitted that this is true of a large class of such statements, a class encompassing tautologies and duplicative identity statements of the form of (1). And the objectual analysis implies that all identity statements are of this class.

29 This might be thought to be implied by Kripke's causal-chain picture of reference.

30 G E Moore [1], p. 263.

31 A logically simple property is, roughly, one which can be expressed by a predicate which semantically is neither conjunctive, disjunctive, conditional, nor formed from a simple property by some operation such as world-indexing (*see* chapter five).

32 David Wiggins [3]. *See also* Ledger Wood [1], p. 178, for the claim that 'Identity, conceived as a relation between a thing and itself, is a pseudo-relation'; David Shwayder [1], pp. 24, 28, 36; and John Woods [1].

33 Kripke [2], p. 350.

34 Cf. G J Warnock [1], p. 84.

CHAPTER 2

1 *See* Alfred Tarski [1], p. 60, and Frank Ramsey [1], pp. 16–17.

2 Frege [3].

3 Ibid. p. 56.

4 Ibid.; *see also* Ledger Wood [1].

5 Leonard Linsky [2], p. 22. Unfortunately, many commentators agree on this reading. Included among them are Butchvarov and Michael Dummett.

6 Frege [3], p. 57.

7 *See* Searle [3]. *See also* Ledger Wood [1], p. 178.

8 Frege [3], p. 57.

9 Michael Devitt [1], pp. 9–13. L Johathan Cohen [1] refers to the multiplicity of semantic types connectible with single word types of proper names as the 'versatility' of names, and stresses the importance of this semantic phenomenon.

10 David Wiggins makes this criticism in [3], p. 51. *See also* John Woods [2], p. 85, and William Kneale and Martha Kneale [1], p. 494.

11 I talk of the presuppositions of *sentences* rather than of statements merely for convenience. The presuppositions of a sentence are to be understood here as those of the statement it standardly is (or would be) used to make (in English) in ordinary conversational contexts.

12 *See* Charles Landesman [1], p. 147, and Wiggins [3], p. 70.

13 John Woods [2] claims that 'a = b' and 'a = a' should be given two different analyses.

14 Michael Dummett [1], p. 544.

15 Paul Ziff [1], p. 176, suggests that referring expressions can so work that it is about *both*. In holding this, he seems to be nearly alone.

16 W V Quine [1], p. 221.

17 Woods [2], pp. 87–9, seems to deny this.

CHAPTER 3

1 Of course, not all these principles need be listed by an author presenting the identity relation. For instance, given the principles of symmetry and transitivity, reflexivity follows.

2 John Woods [1], p. 179.

3 Ibid.

4 Baruch Brody [1], p. 10.

5 *See* the discussion at the end of chapter one. What I mean by the distinction between logically simple and logically composite properties should become clearer in chapter five.

6 It has been attempted by some contributors to the ongoing debate concerning what are called 'particularized attributes'. For a recent look at the notion, *see* Jerrold Levinson [1].

7 Brody [1], p. 8.

8 *See*, for example, David Coder [1], pp. 339–43. I should mention here that in a recently published article, Richard Mendelsohn, more than any other commentator I know of, recognises the continuity between Frege's early metalinguistic position and the views elaborated in this later article. *See* Mendelsohn [1].

9 Kripke [2], p. 310.

10 Kripke [3], p. 16.

CHAPTER 4

1 P F Strawson [2], p. 54. *See also* Shwayder [1], p. 36.

2 Shwayder [1] has stated the following: 'Judgements of identity—like existential judgements—are true-or-false without being in any sense descriptive. By "descriptive judgement" I mean the kind of statement we make when we predicate any property or any proper (possibly multiple) relation of one or more objects . . .', p. 22.

3 *See* Shwayder [1], pp. 29–30, and Ruth Barcan Marcus [1], pp. 35–6.

4 *See* chapter one.

5 E J Lemmon [1], p. 160. *See also* Bede Rundle [1], p. 68.

6 See Marcus [1], pp. 35–6. In contrast to Marcus, compare J M Bell [1].

7 By use of the term 'functional', I mean to indicate any aspect of meaning not susceptible of explicit definition.

8 Michael Lockwood [1], p. 205.

9 Exactly what sorts of properties are collated, I shall indicate later in the section.

10 A J Ayer [1], p. 182.

11 Strawson [2], pp. 54–6.

12 Ibid. p. 55.

13 Ibid.

14 Ibid. p. 56.

15 Ibid.

16 Lockwood [1], p. 209. *See also* Roger White [1]. White says: ' "Cicero is Tully" does not convey one piece of information to every English speaker, but it can "convey" information in a variety of ways', and '. . . the information conveyed will differ considerably for different people depending on how they are circumstanced, where they have encountered these names in the past' (p. 173).

17 Keith S Donnellan [1].

18 For a well known critique, *see* Kripke [2].

19 *See* Ayer [1], p. 186; and *also* David Bell [1], pp. 63, 76.

20 Ibid. p. 190. *See* again the quote from Roger White in n. 16 above. After a discussion of proper names in a recent article Peter Carruthers [1] remarks: 'So we can explain the informativeness of an identity-statement, but we shall no longer wish to talk about *the* information content of such a statement. On the contrary, what information such a statement will convey may vary person to person, depending on what information is associated by each person with the names on either side of the identity-sign.' Neither White nor Carruthers has much at all to say about the constraints on how the information may vary, or even about what sorts of information will be involved. This is what I have attempted to adumbrate in the text. A number of recent writers who differ substantially in the details of their accounts of proper names, and who propound very different types of account, nevertheless agree that there must be some association of descriptive information with the standard use of a name, however loose the association or minimal the information might be. *See* Hartry Field [1]; Michael Devitt [1], pp. 130–3; Gareth Evans [1] and Evans' posthumously published book [2], p. 399 and elsewhere; *see also* John Searle [1].

21 John Searle [2], p. 171.

22 Quine [1], p. 222.

23 Ibid.

24 Wittgenstein [1], p. 105.

25 Ibid. p. 107.

26 Butchvarov [1], p. 34. As Tyler Burge [1], p. 354, has said: 'Knowledge about public objects is indeed perspectival. Even in direct perception we see physical objects from one side at a time; and so it is in principle possible to fail to realize that an object, when viewed from one perspective, is the same object as was just seen from another perspective.'

27 Hector-Neri Castañeda [1].

28 Ibid.

29 Butchvarov [1] draws a parallel distinction between, respectively, entities and objects.

30 Butchvarov [2], p. 173.

CHAPTER 5

1 Gareth Evans [2], p. 67.

2 Op. cit. p. 23.

3 Bede Rundle [1], p. 21.
4 Mark Platts [1], pp. 145–50.
5 Gilbert Harman [1], p. 11.
6 Rundle [1], pp. 4, 5.
7 Alvin Plantinga [3], pp. 369–70.
8 D M Armstrong [1].
9 *See,* for example, Dorothy Walsh [1], pp. 241–4.
10 L Johathan Cohen [1], pp. 162–3.
11 Armstrong, op. cit. p. 11.
12 Ibid.
13 Ruth Barcan [2], pp. 12–15. *See also* Wiggins [2], and Kripke [1], pp. 135–6.
14 For published doubts, *see* Brody [1], pp. 126–7. It might be thought that remarks of mine in chapter three applied here would raise doubt about world indexed properties, but this is not so. I raise questions about alleged properties which are supposed to be both logically simple and uniquely instantiable. World-indexed definite descriptions would convey uniquely instantiable properties, but not logically simple ones. A simple property is one which can be expressed by a predicate which semantically is neither conjunctive, disjunctive, conditional, nor formed from a simple predicate by some operation such as world-indexing.

CHAPTER 6

1 Cartwright [1], p. 120.
2 Wiggins [1], p. 5. *See also* Wiggins [4], p. 21.
3 Cartwright, op. cit. p. 133.
4 Wiggins, ibid.
5 Benson Mates [1], p. 153. Russell once wrote: 'Identity is a rather puzzling thing at first sight. When you say "Scott is the author of *Waverley*", you are half-tempted to think there are two people, one of whom is Scott and the other the author of *Waverley*, and they happen to be the same. This is obviously absurd, but that is the sort of way one is always tempted to deal with identity'. *See his* [1], p. 247. May Brodbeck [1] registers her self-consciousness about this form of expression with quotes when she writes: 'In other words, "two" individuals that are numerically one and the same must be qualitatively the same, though the converse does not hold.' *See her* [1], p. 47.
6 *See,* for example, Max Black [1].
7 Shwayder [1], p. 21.
8 Ibid. Compare here Brody [1]. *See especially* pp. 13–14.
9 Marcus [1].
10 By saying only that the 'available form' of the contents of a mental file is that of linguistic representations, we leave open the possibility of giving an ontological account of those contents as either mental or neural items.
11 This is an example used notably by W V Quine [2], pp. 143–4.

12 Ibid. pp. 141–2; and Quine [3], pp. 141–56.
13 Ibid.
14 Marcus [1].
15 Ibid.
16 Wiggins [4], p. 22. The repudiation of Leibniz's Law is a strategy used, for example, by A P Martinich [1] to avoid logical difficulties.

CHAPTER 7

1 Such emendations have been presented by philosophers such as James Corman and Thomas Nagel. *See,* for example, Cornman [1], p. 129, and Nagel [1], pp. 96–111. Compare R Routley and V MacRae [1].
2 Friedrich Waismann [1], p. 93.
3 Ibid. p. 99. Notice that Waismann is not clear concerning whether sentences, or statements, or both serve to make up a language stratum.
4 Ibid. p. 50; *see also* pp. 100, 119. As will become evident, it is just this kind of problem to which the theory of regulative identity purports to be relevant.
5 P F Strawson [1].
6 *See,* for example, John Wisdom [1], p. 219.
7 For detailed discussion of this type of argument, *see* James Corman [2].
8 On meaninglessness and necessary falsehood, *see* Theodore Drange [1], ch. 7, and Edward Erwin [1].
9 As Peter Geach [1] has said: 'What can be truly predicated depends not only on what the subject-term signifies but also on the *modus significandi* of the subject-term', p. 310.

CHAPTER 8

1 Don Garrett [1], p. 84. This criticism originally derives from Robert Fogelin.
2 I am assuming here, for the sake of argument, what may in fact be false. *See* the next chapter.
3 This, of course, will be Kripke's 'weak necessity'.
4 This is true at least of modes admitting of identity statements. And this is what the divine mode must be if the theory is to work.
5 This is a distinction now commonly made.
6 I owe this formulation of the problem to Michael Williams.
7 Austin Farrer [1], p. 28.
8 It is interesting to reflect on the 'neutral monism' of Russell and others in light of this problem.
9 Geach [1], p. 238.
10 Shalom Lappin [1], p. 127. Lappin does not discuss the sort of examples I shall give, and does not offer a description of metaphorical identity such as I shall attempt to provide.
11 Stuart E Rosenbaum [1], and James Cornman [2].

CHAPTER 9

1 Don Cupitt [1], p. 625.
2 John Hick [1], p. 156. Of course, Hick's charge as it stands is infelicitous. 'This square is a circle' is not devoid of meaning; it just cannot standardly be used in English to state anything other than a necessary falsehood.
3 Brian Hebblethwaite [1], p. 86.
4 A D Smith [1], pp. 263–264.
5 Stephan P Schwartz [1].
6 Richard A Norris, Jr [1], p. 81.
7 John McQuarrie [1], p. 13. Unfortunately, in the same article, McQuarrie states, without argument, that 'There is no universal essence that you can call "humanity" . . .' (p. 19).
8 Herbert McCabe and Maurice Wiles [1], p. 552.

Bibliography

Armstrong, D M   [1] *A Theory of Universals: Universals and Scientific Realism, Volume II* (Cambridge: Cambridge University Press, 1978)

Ayer, Alfred Jules [1] Identity and Reference, *Philosophia* **5** (1975)

Barcan, Ruth   *See* Marcus, Ruth Barcan

Bell, David   [1] Frege's *Theory of Judgement* (Oxford: Clarendon Press, 1979)

Bell, J M   [1] Opacity and Identity, *Analysis* **31** (1970)

Black, Max   [1] The Identity of Indiscernibles, *Mind* **LXI** (1952). Reprinted in *Universals and Particulars,* revised edn. Edited by Michael J Loux (Notre Dame: University of Nore Dame Press, 1970)

Brodbeck, May   [1] Mental and Physical: Identity Versus Sameness, *Mind, Matter and Method.* Edited by Paul K Feyeraband and Grover Maxwell (Minneapolis: University of Minnesota Press, 1966)

Brody, Baruch   [1] *Identity and Essence* (Princeton: Princeton University Press, 1980)

Burge, Tyler   [1] Belief *De Re, Journal of Philosophy* **LXXIV** (1977)

Butchvarov, Panayot   [1] *Being Qua Being: A Theory of Identity, Existence, and Predication* (Bloomington: Indiana University Press, 1979)

—— [2] Identity, *Contemporary Perspectives in the Philosophy of Language.* Edited by Peter A French: Theodore E Uehling Jr; and Howard K Wettstein (Minneapolis: University of Minnesota Press, 1979)

Carruthers, Peter   [1] Understanding Names, *Philosophical Quarterly* **33** (1983)

Cartwright, Richard   [1] Identity and Substitutivity, *Identity and Individuation.* Edited by Milton K Munitz (New York: New York University Press, 1971)

—— [2] Indiscernibility Principles, *Midwest Studies in Philosophy, Volume IV: Studies in Metaphysics.* Edited by Peter A French, Theodore E Uehling, Jr, and Howard K Wettstein (Minneapolis: University of Minnesota Press, 1979)

Castañeda, Hector-Neri   [1] Identity and Sameness, *Philosophia* **5** (1975)

Cohen, L Jonathan   [1] The individuation of Proper Names, *Philosophical Subjects.* Edited by Zak Van Straaten (Oxford: Clarendon Press, 1980)

Cornman, James W   [1] The Identity of Mind and Body, *The Mind-Brain Identity Theory.* Edited by C V Borst (London: Macmillan, 1970)

—— [2] *Materialism and Sensations* (New Haven: Yale University Press, 1971)

—— [2] Mind-Body Identity: Cross-Category or Not?, *Philosophical Studies* **32** (1977)

—— [3] *Perception, Common Sense, and Science* (New Haven: Yale University Press, 1975)

—— [4] Types, Categories, and Nonsense, *Studies in Logical Theory.* American Philosophical Quarterly Monograph Series, no. 2. Edited by Nicholas Rescher (Oxford: Basil Blackwell, 1968)

Cupitt, Don   [1] The Finality of Christ, *Theology* **78** (December 1975)

Donnellan, Keith S   [1] Proper Names and Identifying Descriptions'. *Semantics of Natural Language,* 2nd edn. Edited by Donald Davidson and Gilbert Harman (Dordrecht: D Reidel, 1972)

—— [2] Reference and Definite Descriptions, *Naming, Necessity, and Natural Kinds.* Edited by Stephen P Schwartz (Ithaca: Cornell University Press, 1977)

Drange, Theodore   [1] *Type Crossings* (The Hague: Mouton, 1966)

Dummett, Michael   [1] *Frege: Philosophy of Language* (New York: Harper and Row, 1973)

Erwin, Edward   [1] *The Concept of Meaninglessness* (Baltimore: Johns Hopkins Press, 1970)

Evans, Gareth   [1] The Causal Theory of Names, *Naming, Necessity, and Natural Kinds.* Edited by Stephen P Schwartz (Ithaca: Cornell University Press, 1977)

—— [2] *The Varieties of Reference.* Edited by John McDowell (Oxford: Clarendon Press, 1982)

Feldman, Fred   [1] Leibniz and Leibniz's Law, *Philosophical Review* **79** (1970)

Field, Hartry   [1] Logic, Meaning, and Conceptual Role, *Journal of Philosophy* **LXXIV** (1977)

Fitch, G W   [1] Are There Necessary A Priori Truths?, *Philosophical Studies* **30** (1976)

Frege, Gottlob   [1] *Conceptual Notation and Related Articles.* Translated and edited by Terrell Ward Bynum (Oxford: Clarendon Press, 1972)

—— [2] *Philosophical and Mathematical Correspondence.* Edited by Gottfried Gabriel, Hans Hermes, Friedrich Kambartel, Christian Theil, and Albert Veraart. Abridged for the English edition by Brian McGuiness, and translated by Hans Kaal (Oxford: Basil Blackwell, 1979)

—— [3] On Sense and Reference, *Translations from the Philosophical Writings of Gottlob Frege.* Edited by Peter Geach and Max Black (Oxford: Basil Blackwell, 1966)

Fodor, Jerry   [1] *Psychological Explanation* (New York: Random House, 1968)

Garrett, Don   [1] Identity, Necessity, and the Mind-Body Problem. Unpublished PhD dissertation (Yale University, 1979)

Geach, Peter   [1] *Logic Matters* (Berkeley: University of California Press, 1980)

Grandy, Richard   [1] A Definition of Truth for Theories with Intensional Definite Description Operators, *Journal of Philosophical Logic* **1** (1972)

Grice, H P   [1] Vacuous Names, *Words and Objections.* Edited by Donald Davidson and Jaako Hintikka (Dodrecht: D Reidel, 1969)

Griffin, Nicholas [1] *Relative Identity* (Oxford: Clarendon Press, 1977)

Hacking, Ian [1] On the Reality of Existence and Identity, *Canadian Journal of Philosophy* **VIII** (1978)

Harman, Gilbert [1] Meaning and Semantics, *Semantics and Philosophy.* Edited by Milton K Munitz and Peter Unger (New York: New York University Press, 1974)

Hebblethwaite, Brian [1] Incarnation: the Essence of Christianity?, *Theology* **80** (1977)

Hick, John [1] Jesus and the World Religions, *The Myth of God Incarnate.* Edited by John Hick (London: SCM Press, 1977)

Katz, Bernard D [1] The Identity of Indiscernibles Revisited, *Philosophical Studies* **44** (1983)

Kneale, William and Kneale, Martha [1] *History of Logic* (Oxford: Oxford University Press, 1962)

Kripke, Saul [1] Identity and Necessity, *Identity and Individuation.* Edited by Milton K Munitz (New York: New York University Press, 1971)

―― [2] Naming and Necessity, *Semantics of Natural Language*, 2nd edn. Edited by Donald Davidson and Gilbert Harman (Dordrecht: D Reidel, 1972)

―― [3] Speaker's Reference and Semantic Reference, *Contemporary Perspectives in the Philosophy of Language.* Edited by Peter French, Theodore Uehling, and Howard Wettstein (Minneapolis: University of Minnesota Press, 1979)

Landesman, Charles [1] *Discourse and Its Presuppositions* (New Haven: Yale University Press, 1972)

Lappin, Shalom [1] *Sorts, Ontology, and Metaphor* (New York: Walter de Gruyter, 1981)

Lemmon, E J [1] *Beginning Logic* (Indianapolis: Hackett, 1978)

Levinson, Jerrold [1] The Particularization of Attributes, *Australasian Journal of Philosophy* **58** (1980)

Linsky, Leonard [1] *Names and Descriptions* (Chacago: University of Chicago Press, 1977)

―― [2] *Referring* (London: Routledge and Kegan Paul, 1967)

Lockwood, Michael [1] Identity and Reference, *Identity and Individuation.* Edited by Milton K Munitz (New York: New York University Press, 1971)

Marcus, Ruth Barcan [1] Does the Principle of Substitutivity Rest on a Mistake? *The Logical Enterprise.* Edited by Alan Ross Anderson; Ruth Barcan Marcus; and Richard M Martin (New Haven: Yale University Press, 1975)

―― [2] The Identity of Individuals in a Strict Functional Calculus of Second Order, *Journal of Symbolic Logic* **12** (1947)

Martinich, A P [1] Identity and Trinity, *Journal of Religion* (1978)

McCabe, Herbert and Wiles, Maurice [1] The Incarnation: An Exchange, *New Blackfriars* **58** (1977)

McQuarrie, John The Humility of God, *The Myth/Truth of God Incarnate.* Edited by Durstan R McDonald (Wilton, Connecticut: Moorehouse-Barlow, 1979)

Mendelsohn, Richard L [1] Frege's *Begriffsschrift* Theory of Identity, *Journal of the History of Philosophy* **XX** (1982)
—— [2] Rigid Designation and Informative Identity Sentences, *Midwest Studies in Philosophy, Volume IV: Studies in Metaphysics.* Edited by Peter A French, Theodore E Uehling, Jr, and Howard K Wettstein (Minneapolis: University of Minnesota Press, 1979)
Moore, G E [1] Identity, *The Commonplace Book of G E Moore.* Edited by Casimir Lewy (London: George Allen and Unwin, 1962)
Nagel, Thomas [1] Physicalism, *Materialism and the Mind-Body Problem.* Edited by David M Rosenthal (Englewood Cliffs: Prentice-Hall, 1971)
Norris, Richard A (Jr) [1] Interpreting the Doctrine of the Incarnation, *The Myth/Truth of God Incarnate.* Edited by Durstan R McDonald (Wilton, Connecticut: Moorehouse-Barlow, 1979)
Perry, John [1] Identity. Unpublished PhD dissertation (Cornell University, 1968)
Plantinga, Alvin [1] The Boethian Compromise, *American Philosophical Quarterly* **15** (1978)
—— [2] *The Nature of Necessity* (Oxford: Clarendon Press, 1974)
—— [3] World and Essence, *Universals and Particulars: Readings in Ontology,* revised edn. Edited by Michael J Loux (Notre Dame: University of Notre Dame Press, 1976)
Platts, Mark [1] *Ways of Meaning: An Introduction to a Philosophy of Language* (London: Routledge and Kegan Paul, 1979)
Quine, W. V. [1] *Methods of Logic,* 3rd edn. (New York: Holt, Rinehart, & Winston, 1972)
—— [2] Reference and Modality. *From a Logical Point of View,* 2nd edn (New York: Harper and Row, 1960)
—— [3] *Word and Object* (Cambridge: M.I.T. Press, 1960)
Ramsey, Frank P [1] *The Foundations of Mathematics and Other Logical Essays.* Edited by R B Braithwaite (Totowa, N J: Littlefield, Adams, 1965)
Rosenbaum, Stuart E [1] The Property Objection and the Principle of Identity, *Philosophical Studies* **32** (1977)
Routley, Richard and MacRae, Vera [1] On the Identity of Sensations and Physiological Occurrences, *American Philosophical Quarterly* **3** (1966)
Rundle, Bede [1] *Grammar in Philosophy* (Oxford: Clarendon Press, 1979)
Russell, Bertrand [1] The Philosophy of Logical Atomism, *Logic and Knowledge.* Edited by Robert C Marsh (London: George Allen and Unwin, 1956)
Schwartz, Stephen P [1] Natural Kinds and Nominal Kinds, *Mind* **89** (1980)
Scott, Dana [1] Existence and Description in Formal Logic, *Bertrand Russell: Philosopher of the Century.* Edited by Ralph Schoenman (London: George Allen and Unwin, 1967)
Smith, A D [1] God's Death, *Theology* **80** (1977)
Searle, John R [1] Proper Names and Intentionality, *Pacific Philosophical Quarterly* **63** (1982)

—— [2] *Speech Acts: An Essay in the Philosophy of Language* (Cambridge: Cambridge University Press, 1969)

—— [3] Proper Names, *Philosophical Logic*. Edited by P F Strawson (Oxford: Oxford University Press, 1967)

Shwayder, D S   [1] *"="* Mind n.s. **65** (1956)

Sommers, Fred   [1] Predicability, *Philosophy in America*. Edited by Max Black (Ithaca: Cornell University Press, 1965)

—— [2] Types and Ontology, *Philosophical Logic*. Edited by P F Strawson (Oxford: Oxford University Press, 1967)

Stalnaker, Robert   [1] Propositions, *Issues in the Philosophy of Language*. Edited by Alfred F Mackay and Daniel D Merrill. Proceedings of the 1972 Oberlin Colloquium in Philosophy (New Haven: Yale University Press, 1976)

Strawson, P. F.   [1] *Individuals: An Essay in Descriptive Metaphysics* (London: Methuen, 1959)

—— [2] *Subject and Predicate in Logic and Grammar* (London: Methuen, 1974)

Tarski, Alfred   [1] *Introduction to Logic and to the Methodology of the Deductive Sciences* (New York: Oxford University Press, 1965)

Tichy, Pavel   [1] Kripke on Necessity A Posteriori, *Philosophical Studies* **43** (1983)

Tye, Michael   [1] The Puzzle of Hesperus and Phosphorus, *Australasian Journal of Philosophy* **56** (1978)

Waismann, Friedrich   [1] Language Strata, *How I See Philosophy*. Edited by R Harre (New York: St Martin's Press, 1968)

Walsh, Dorothy   [1] Occam's Razor: A Principle of Intellectual Elegance, *American Philosophical Quarterly* **16** (1979)

Warnock, G. J.   [1] Metaphysics in Logic, *Essays in Conceptual Analysis*. Edited by Antony Flew (London: Macmillan, 1960)

White, Alan   [1] Mind-Brain Analogies, *Canadian Journal of Philosophy* **1** (1972)

—— [2] Propositions and Sentences, *Bertrand Russell Memorial Volume*. Edited by George W Roberts (London: George Allen and Unwin, 1979)

White, Roger   [1] Wittgenstein on Identity, *Proceedings of the Aristotelian Society* new series **LXVIII** (1978)

Wiggins, David   [1] *Identity and Spatio-temporal Continuity* (Oxford: Basil Blackwell, 1967)

—— [2] Identity, Necessity, and Physicalism, *Philosophy of Logic*. Edited by Stephen Korner (Oxford: Basil Blackwell, 1976)

—— [3] Identity Statements, *Analytical Philosophy: Second Series*. Edited by R J Butler (New York: Barnes and Noble, 1965)

—— [4] *Sameness and Substance* (Cambridge, Mass: Harvard University Press, 1980)

Wisdom, John   [1] Things and Persons, *Philosophy and Psycho-analysis* (Oxford: Basil Blackwell, 1957)

Wittgenstein, Ludwig   [1] *Tractatus Logico-Philosophicus*. Translated by D F Pears and B F McGuiness (London: Routledge and Kegan Paul, 1961)

Wood, Ledger   [1] *The Analysis of Knowledge* (London: George Allen and Unwin, 1940)

Woods, John   [1] Essentialism, Self-Identity, and Quantifying In, *Identity and Individuation*. Edited by Milton K Munitz (New York: New York University Press, 1971)

—— [2] Identity and Modality, *Philosophia* **5** (1975)

Ziff, Paul   [1] *Semantic Analysis* (Ithaca: Cornell University Press, 1960)